The Obama Tribe Explorer

James Martin's Biography

Mark Pullicino

First published in Great Britain in 2016 by MPI publishing, Great Britain, A catalogue record for this title is available from the British Library.
ISBN 978-0-9544906-6-9

This is a revised, extended and refocused version of the earlier publication: James Martin, The Maltese Adventurer, Mark Pullicino; published by MPI Publishing in 2013
ISBN:978-99957-0-584-8

Facebook.com@ObamaHistory
Twitter #ObamaExplorer
Email: mpipublishing@aol.com

Prologue

"Utterly fascinating reading to any who want to understand Africa." ***Midwest Book Review***

"This is a delightful book that instead of giving the bare facts also provides the context." ***The Independent***

"Accounts of East African Tribes and British Colonial policy are very useful and pertinent." ***The Times (Malta)***

"Amazing what James Martin achieved despite being seriously dyslexic." ***Gerry Delany***

Dr. Mark Pullicino was born in Malta and left to complete his upbringing in East Africa, (St. Mary's School, Nairobi) he gained degrees from UK universities Aberdeen /Engineering), Edinburgh (Business), US university Wayne State / Educational Psychology and a PhD in Social Sciences from the Technische Universitaet-Berlin.

He lectured at Lancaster and Robert Gordon's Universities. After a successful career in management consulting with multinational companies, he now lives with his wife in Malta.

His books include:

- *Sozio-psychologische Auswirkungen importierter, entwickelter Industrietechnologie*, TU, Berlin, (1975)
- *Process Think: Leading to Change and Innovation*, London, (2003),
- *Opening Africa* (co-authored with P Pullicino, (2008),
- *James Martin, The Maltese Explorer*, (2013) (This is earlier version of revised "The Obama Tribe Explorer")

.

Contents

Photographs: **318**

There is often one defining moment of a person's life, very often he or she doesn't realize the importance of that short incident. Indeed it sometimes may take years or even centuries for the significance of that deed to become clear and understood.

In 1883 the first white man made contact with the Luo tribe of Western Kenya, the people of the first Black President, the 44th, of the United States, Barak Obama.

This moment brought together amazing characters and situations of adventure and societies, which although may have seemed a casual handshake, in fact were the special catalysts that drove future events. It is no coincidence that the first black President came from Western Kenya and not the slums of Harlem, or among the followers of Malcolm X or of Martin Luther King.

This book tells you why.

.

This is the true story of the adventurous life of James Martin, who had made that first handshake "for President Obama".

His actual name was Antonio Martini, Anglecised to James or Jimmy Martin. He was born just outside Valletta in 1857 and spent his formative childhood years in Malta, an island in the middle of the Mediterranean Sea. At the age of sixteen, having learned the trade of sail-making, he embarked on a life at sea, eventually landing in Zanzibar where he began his adventures as an East Africa explorer, a mere seven years after the African exploits and life of David Livingstone had come to an end.

Although the basic, amazing story of Martin is true, with the shipwrecks, journeys and other feats of his life documented in various sources, I have tried at the same time to tie his life into the context of, not only his state of mind but also the places, culture, politics, events and times in which he lived. In doing this, I have included references to my own ancestors who would have helped shape life in Malta during Martin's lifetime. I have thus fictionalised some aspects of his biography, in that I have linked his story to other contemporary occurrences to make his childhood and formative years, as well as his adult environment in Africa, more understandable, interesting and engaging, by understanding the context of the time.

The previous published version of his biography, generated several comments from readers. One medical doctor remarked: 'Martin was illiterate, but you know, the description of his behavior shows that he must have been dyslexic.' Here, also, I have tried to give his apparent dyslexia the context it deserves and perhaps, by doing so, answer critics that dismissed him as "just an illiterate". I give a brief outline of the significance of this condition in an introduction before beginning the biography, which is a reworking and extension of my original book.

Introduction
Dyslexia

In the early nineteenth century, western religious philosophies tended to give explanations for states of the mind. The actions and thoughts that were good were reinforced; those that were bad were condemned. Apparently nonsensical thoughts or images were rarely rationalised but were covered over, rejected or ignored, leaving fear that the mind harboured evils that were part of us and were often pushing to get out. That must not be allowed to happen at any cost: if it did, it could spell disaster, and the end of a person's moral and social life. Worry, fear, uncertainty, guilt and inhibition were the resulting dominant drivers. Change, innovation and progress were very slow to happen.

By the late nineteenth century, the scientific study of the human mind had begun to explain these apparent nonsensical thoughts. People such as William James, Hermann von Helmholtz and Charles

Peirce, to name but a few, were the pioneers. Freud's influential book on the interpretation of dreams was yet to be published, but it would give these images in the mind a different meaning, structure and purpose. Light was shed on the dark jungle of the subconscious. Psychoanalysis began to give an awareness of where thoughts and images came from, and that rather than being our controlling masters, these thoughts and images were able to help us. In the 1890s, Breuer and Freud began to study conditions such as hysteria and attempted to find ways to cure them. However, lesser occurrences to do with the mind remained in a black box labeled 'unknown'. The knowledge map of the mind was still mostly blank, with wild, savage notions of what went on in the interior, being the status quo.

The term 'dyslexia' was coined in Germany in 1887 by Rudolf Berlin of Stuttgart. Today it is a description for general learning and reading difficulties; there are over seventy detailed categories of dyslexia, including dyscalculia (maths disability) and dyspraxia (motor or movement-learning difficulties). Autism and Asperger's syndrome are conditions that also have some aspects in common with dyslexia. Even today, nearly 140 years later, the dynamics of the condition are still not fully understood.

What we do know is that early visual impulses go through the eye and are turned upside down by the eye's lens and projected on the back of the retina before moving into the network of the neural grid with its crossing nerve paths (rather like a fishing net tied by nodes or neurons). The first neuron activated sends impulses through connector synapses to other neurons located in different sense zones or sections, also known as axon hillocks.

When someone points at a cat and says 'cat', this sound bite shoots from the ears into the neural grid and establishes itself in a sound memory section and at the same time links up with the visual image. It is only after repeated runs of this exercise that the visual image 'cat' and the sound bite 'cat' develop connecting neural pathways. Further use of this link enables the establishment of the three elements of information and the means with which to tie them together:

- the real object of the cat
- the image of the real object of the cat – a picture
- the sound of the word that invokes both the real object and the image of the real object.

The pathways become established, or trodden, by repetition and are thus fixed. It is an inability to make these link-ups, or rather some of these associations, that causes dyslexia.

The next stage is where more complex concepts of time, sequencing, location and orientation are formed. All these need to be established, or at least initiated, before the main benefit of our civilisation's development is embedded: learning how to read and write – that is, understanding the concept and sound of letters and then recreating them in writing. Here is where the dyslexic begins to develop more problems. To better understand the process, we need to look at the different ways in which we think.

There are two ways in which our minds and thought processes deal with incoming stimuli: the first is *non-verbal conceptualisation*; the second, *verbal conceptualisation.*

Non-verbal conceptualisation means that thought processes produce images that are mental pictures. It is the first way we think and input images to our mind. A child combines images with sound bites when beginning to talk, using non-verbal conceptualisation. The other thought process, verbal conceptualisation, evolves and increases as we learn to read and write and is determined by the structure of a language. One process involves the linking up of images, pictures and sounds; the other involves linking up letters and words with their meaning and also their sound. Verbal conceptualisation follows a more linear pattern, rather like reading to yourself. As you read this page you are probably using verbal conceptualisation. Verbal thinking is much slower than non-verbal thinking; in fact, it can be hundreds of times slower. Most people use a mixture of verbal and non-verbal thinking.

Dyslexics, however, have the gift of being predominantly exceptional non-verbal thinkers (they think in images). The neural pathways that facilitate this thinking are well defined and utilised, and can be very fast; this is almost like the gift of intuition, of being able to see things shaped in the future and reorganise things in the present. Such people are able to change thoughts into reality. Some experts believe that famous people who have been helped by this dyslexic advantage include Leonardo da Vinci with his picture details, Alexander Graham Bell with his telephone vision, Albert Einstein with his relativity images, and Walt Disney with his cartoons. More contemporaneous is the singer Florence Welsh (of Florence and the Machine) with her images of sound and her musical abilities. All these people were able to take advantage of their gift and turn it into something worthwhile – an expertise for which they became famous.

The dyslexic's mind makes faster connections then most people's, with more of the brain coming alive. The multitude of images created, however, has a downside: inability to choose which of these many image to act on creates a sort of overload and the mind becomes indecisive and passive. Sometimes these images do not reflect reality, and when this discrepancy is realised, it comes as a shock to the dyslexic, creating, at worst, panic attacks.

This condition of James Martin's mind is key to understanding some of his behaviours, motivations and success. A chemist needs to understand basic elements; an engineer, the forces of physics and mathematics; a biographer, the natural make-up and psychology of the mind and the environment in which it lives – both nature and nurture.

1 The drowning

The Royal Geographical Society, London, in its *Geographical Journal*, Vol. LXVI, No.1 (July 1925), published an obituary of James Martin (alias Antonio Martini). An extract from the obituary reads:

This man stands out as the greatest caravan leader of the day when the lives of Lugard and his staff in Uganda were absolutely dependent on the periodic dispatch of stores transported from Mombasa – a trifling walk of 800 miles.

Martin was a Maltese by birth and a sailor by trade. A man of no education but possessing great natural gifts and no mean ability, his connection with the East Coast of Africa commences about 1880 or perhaps earlier. He was a hand on a sailing vessel which was wrecked in the Red Sea …

It was a pitch-dark night, with screaming winds. He was tossed about in the tempestuous sea and wallowed in what seemed to be bottomless troughs between the waves which then lifted him up to be slapped by the curling wave-tops. Unable even to see the sky or the stars to gain some sort of orientation, anyone could have resigned themselves to a miserable death, alone, wet and cold. James Martin had to rise to this exceptional occasion with courage and faith in himself, or he would go down.

The shipwrecked sailor clung desperately to his spar and for the umpteenth time checked, by an almost automatic movement, the end-frayed rope which had providently been entangled with the spar when he grabbed it in the water and which he had wound around his chest, and under his armpits, as his first reaction to seek safety from drowning. Indeed, without that lifeline he would long have been parted from his improvised raft. His sudden contact with the dark black sea had been a shock, but it had also triggered his swimming reflexes and he was quickly able to stop his descent and swim upwards, breaking through to the surface of the water to gasp fresh air and breathe again. He was a good swimmer, having learned at a very early age, but even the best swimmer would not have survived for long in that turbulent sea without some means of support. He had been in the water for probably four or five hours in pitch darkness since that frightening moment when he was washed off the deck by a gigantic rogue wave that struck as the ship was heeled on her beam ends. Part of the mainmast had snapped and various pieces of deck equipment had been wrenched off and cast into the sea before the vessel itself disappeared in the darkness ahead. It must have been the combination of that vicious north-easterly wind and the contrary buffeting waves – an incredible moment, in which the forces of nature seemed to conspire. The jerk of the wind against the sails above and the drive of the waves from below had twisted the wooden boat in opposite directions. That did it. Every material has its limit, not least old wood. Every sailor knows that a wind more from the stern than from the bow is more dangerous, less controllable. The captain couldn't have been thinking straight. Martin was not sure whether the ship had righted herself and sailed on or whether she had foundered. There was no way of telling. But then, just as he was cursing his bad luck in the darkness, he bumped against a larger spar that had broken away from the mast with part of the rigging. Now he was miserable and very cold, with aching limbs, but he was alive.

With the coming of dawn the storm seemed to abate. The gusts of wind, low over the surface of the sea, were less strong, and the waves had lost something of their whiplash. This part of the Red Sea was usually prone not to high, daunting waves but to shorter, more punchy ones every bit as dangerous. Of course, the North winds ran right down the narrow sea to the south, building up dangerous momentum as they moved. The sky was still leaden, with low, heavy grey cloud, and did not promise any quick relief. He felt as if he had been in the water for days, and as his strength weakened so did his recollection of time and events. His mind kept wandering back to the past. He examined what he had done wrong to get into this situation. It didn't seem fair. He didn't know where he was, and his vision of things seemed to swirl around his head. He felt disoriented and insecure, feelings his mind had encountered before, only now they were so much more desperate. When he closed his eyes, the focus of his inner vision seemed to spin around and then move outside his head, so that even though his eyes were shut he could see his own wretched body, as if he were hovering gently above it. He saw what a pitiful state he was in: wet and clinging to the spar for dear life, with all the ship's debris around him in the choppy, unfriendly sea. His mind's eye was tempted to turn upwards towards what appeared to be a bright light in the sky. It offered an easy pathway out: warmth, relaxation, rest.

He opened his eyes briefly and thought he saw a glimmer of dawn on the distant horizon line, and the shape of something dark silhouetted there. He wasn't sure if it was real or a dream, but it gave him hope.

2 First sparks fade

Antonio Martini was born in Marsa, Malta, in 1857, in a small village by the sea within the complex of bays of the Valletta harbour, to a Maltese mother and father. His name was changed to the English 'James Martin' after he left Malta and began working on British ships. James's father, a seaman, is believed to have emigrated from Italy in his youth, and based himself in the port village though spending much of his time at sea. The family lived in a small flat-roofed limestone house, down a narrow side road. It was just a few rooms on the ground floor, with a courtyard, and there were neighbours above. James's mother, Maria, had a typical olive-coloured Mediterranean complexion, with dark eyes and slightly curly thick black hair, over which she usually wore a traditional white scarf. Her blouse and ankle-length skirt were generally covered by a work pinafore and her rough, cracked-skinned feet protected only by a pair of well-worn open sandals. She had a quick smile, especially when reminded of the birth of her children, and her laughter lines showed, but her forehead would also wrinkle at the thought of the children she had lost, at birth or later from disease. Laughter and sorrow went hand in hand for this poor family.

There was cause for hope when the first indications baby James gave his mother were of a bright and alert child, healthy and clever. As he wasn't her first child, she could read the little gestures and signs and make comparisons. The pride she felt when he could walk before other children of his age she kept to herself. He was a 'knowing' boy and seemed able to perceive things, such as where some particular object was when his mother had forgotten. He was quick to start talking too, and was always curious; he seemed to tire of a toy quickly, eager to move on to the next thing. Above all, he learned to smile and then laugh at an early age. He was high maintenance in that he needed to be kept occupied. His mother was soon busy with her next child and had less time and attention for James, but she felt sure that he would be okay. James's parents were both illiterate, so there was little stimulus from the family to educate him. However, his mother increasingly entertained the thought that James was the son who would change the family's fortunes. Unlike many other mothers, she formed a bond with her son that was loving but not possessive, so he felt secure but was free of the psychological pressures that often stunt the potential of children. James's natural abilities were allowed room to grow.

James had attended the local *skola tan-nuna* (nursery school) up to the age of seven, where he was taught games, folk tales, nursery rhymes and prayers, all mixed into one. His initial progress was good and his mother's judgment appeared justified: he seemed a gifted child. Despite the lack of any decent educational provision, the kindergarten did, as the children got older, try to instill the basics of counting and numbers and briefly introduced reading. So the rudiments were taught, and those who were able could climb onto the first rung of the ladder of literacy. It would have been expected that James, who appeared to be one of the brightest, would pick up the numerals, and learn to read a little. That was not, however, the case. He showed no aptitude at all, and in fact was most disruptive when numbers were the topic. He would normally not have got much of an education anyway, but his lack of interest closed this door on him completely.

His mother, realising that he was not happy in school and wanting to protect him, thought it better that he should train for a job as soon as possible. Anything that might relate to an unusual mental condition was taboo then, and not talked about. So the early promise James had shown did not materialise. His mother's brief hope that she had a bright, clever son who would rescue the family was dashed – but that was life. No surprises, no miracles. James's last year at school was at the age of about seven. His mother, Maria, seemed to be always busy, either looking after younger children or struggling with the effects or after-effects of pregnancy; a couple of her children died at birth. She thus had less time for James, and this enabled him to do pretty much as he pleased. He had, from an early age, learned to cope without his mother or father. He constantly had something going on with one of his friends and spent most of his time outdoors.

What happened to James at this time was partly a consequence of his dyslexia. The visual impulses in his mind were not able to link up to produce a viable image; they were confused, all over the place, and this affected his behaviour. In that moment of need, there was no one who understood or could help him slowly to establish the links in his mind that he was unable to make; nothing to give him a guide through his confusion or a helping hand to control his active mind. In those times and in that place, things couldn't have been expected to turn out any other way. The knowledge and support were simply not there. The country's educational structure was non-existent – a disgrace in itself and part of a much wider political struggle. The British had been administering Malta for over fifty years, but barely any semblance of an education system had been implemented. Not only was the state of educational affairs poor, but many people couldn't in any case afford to send their children to such schools as there were, because the fees were beyond them. Probably not much more than five per cent of the population actually went to school at all. So James's hopes of a good future were smothered both by the structure of his mind and by the deficiencies of the society and times in which he lived.

The local priest sometimes came to the house and talked to James's mother about, among other things, her children's education.

'If not the girls, then send your boys to the local school, or at least your most gifted son, James,' he would try to persuade her.

'We can hardly afford bread, let alone schooling,' Maria told him. The baker had said the high price of bread was due to the ever increasing taxes put on by the British Administration. 'And if we send one boy to school we have to send them all.'

James felt deep inside that he would have liked to learn to read and write, and that it was an injustice that he was unable to do so. Although he had the essentials for making a living, and didn't really go hungry, he felt that he needed more. He longed for recognition and self-respect, and he also instinctively wanted to understand what was happening in his mind. Mostly, though, he got on with doing the things he liked and learning all about them. One of these was sailing ships, a passion he shared with his father.

3 Ships, sails and skills

James Martin pushed his head over the thick yellow limestone bastion walls and looked down into the blue expanse of the Grand Harbour. Now a grown boy, he was at the harbour front promenade not far from the old Customs House and had come to see the latest ships that had arrived, as well as the British Mediterranean fleet. His father was a sailor and had left on another of his many trips from the same place. Family goodbyes were never easy, and that last one had seemed even harder. James expected his father back any day and wished he could be back sooner. He looked around at the ships in anticipation. Always fascinated by the big ships anchored here, James knew what most of them were. It was magic to him – all those flags and sails caught his imagination. He got most of his information about them from his father, who always answered his questions and told him tales of adventure and far-off countries. But it seemed to James that he never had enough time to ask all the questions he wanted to ask before his father was off on his next trip.

The Suez Canal had opened just three years previously, in 1869, and now that many more ships were passing through Malta on their way to the Far East, Valletta had, in a very short time, become a leading world harbour. Probably the island's best natural resource, the huge harbour was categorised by some as one of the wonders of the world, mainly because from the bastion walls you could look right out into every corner of the harbour and see what shipping activities were going on -– it was a bit like being in a control tower, or in a vast theatre. The harbour had never been so full with every kind of ship as it was today, and James wondered where they were from and what adventures they had been a part of; each one evoked exciting images in his mind. That was the moment when he said to himself that he would definitely go to sea, as soon as he could, probably in one of those magnificent three-masted ships. From his vantage point he could see that there were mainly sailing ships in the harbour, some like the great clippers that occasionally (although rarely) came in; but he noticed that steamships were becoming more commonplace, and that the most impressive of these were the latest iron steamships. There were also some ships that used sails yet were steamships at the same time.

James spotted one that was just coming into the harbour: three masts, with a smallish funnel placed between the middle and the aft mast. A trail of dark grey smoke could be seen puffing out. It was under sail and the wind, a reasonable (Force 4) north-west breeze, required just nine of its full complement of nineteen white sails. Only one of the three jibs, the front one, was up, but this was essential as it helped in steering the ship, pointing its nose in the right direction. The ship was on a starboard broad reach keeping to the northern side of the wide harbour. It then swung round, before reaching Fort Saint Angelo, into the starboard wind: not a jybe, as that manoeuvre would be dangerous in the harbour area, with so many booms and masts. The sails were tightened up for the last time, and as the boat headed into the wind and towards the main Valletta wharf, below the massive 40-metre-high fortification bastions built by La Vallette, the ship continued round and turned right to the wind's direction; the sails began to flap, and only then were they dropped. James even heard the captain shout 'Down sails'. He pretty much knew the order in which they would pull the sails down: first the main sails to reduce the power, and lastly the jibs. It happened so fast. The ship was now almost like a skeleton, with all the rigging showing and without those beautiful sails. It probably did the last 50 yards to the moorings under steam power or momentum alone. The mooring process, with two small rowing dinghies bringing the ropes attached to the buoys towards the ship where they were hauled aboard, cleated and tied down, was fascinating. The ship was safely tied on to a fore buoy and then also on to an aft rope to a mooring to stop it from swinging round. Everyone seemed to know their job, and it went like clockwork. James was captivated.

The ship was, in fact, very similar to the now legendary *Royal Charter*. The association made James think of his friend Pawlu Ruggier, whose uncle was the renowned sailor Guze Ruggier. Guze was known to be a modest man, but James's father had told him many times that he was a world hero, the bravest Maltese sailor of them all – and they were all brave, like his father. Only last summer James had visited Pawlu at his home in nearby Birgu and had actually been met Guze. With his large beard and thick, slightly greying hair, Guze had a friendly smile and after being prompted by Pawlu showed the boys the gold medal given to him by the Royal National Life Boat Institution in Liverpool, and read out to them the citation 'To Joe Rogers, for gallantry in saving life'.

'It was nothing really,' said Guze. 'You would have done the same if you'd had to.'

'Why does it say "Joe Rogers" and not "Guze Ruggier"?' asked James, always ready to make a point or pick out an anomaly.

'Well,' laughed Guze, 'that's the English name they gave me when I first worked on a ship. It made it easier for them to write my name, and easier for me to get paid. "Rogers" was the nearest name they had to "Ruggier".' He lifted his eyebrows and opened his hands with his palms facing up. 'I suppose it was fine by me – it made it easier to get on with the others.' He chuckled to himself, accepting the degradation of the name change. 'It was just over ten years ago now, and I remember it as if it were yesterday …' Then Guze told his story once more to an attentive wide-eyed audience.

He had been a sailor on the *Royal Charter* that fateful night,[1] on 26 October 1859, when James would have been two years old. It was in the last hour of its long three-month journey to Liverpool, carrying hundreds of passengers and laden with large quantities of gold bullion, as ingots or in coins, which it had brought from Australia, where the voyage began. The gold rush there was in full swing at the time and the British market wanted the gold that was mined Down Under. Once the precious cargo was landed the captain would be assured of his fortune; it was part of the transport deal. The passengers were so close to home that the rough weather seemed at first bearable. They would soon be with their loved ones. The thought kept them calm and quiet, but they were still excited.

They had already passed the north-west tip of Anglesey, and on a clear day Liverpool would have been almost in sight. Today, a wicked north-easterly wind was blowing up. The captain continued for a while on the starboard tack, and when he thought he had the angle to beat straight into Liverpool, he shouted, 'Ready to go about to port, lee hoo,' and round the ship went into a north-easterly bearing. No sooner had he tacked than the wind, instead of getting lighter, as he had expected, turned into a Force 9 gale. It began to push the ship away from the Liverpool bearing, towards the rocky coast of north Wales. Attempts to stop the drift with anchor lines failed, as did the chopping off of sails and rigging to reduce the area that the gale could catch, and the limited power of the propeller couldn't stop the ship being wrecked just short of the cliffs south of Dulas Bay. Distress flares were sent out and seen in the nearby village of Moelfre, but conditions were too bad for the local lifeboat to venture out. The wooden ship was stuck on the rocks about 50 metres from the cliffs, continually pounded by huge waves. People on the shore watched this drama unfold, with no sign of help coming. Nor did they feel that they should take any initiative. It wasn't really their affair, and even if they'd wanted to help (which they didn't feel inclined to) there was nothing they could do: they hadn't been trained for a situation like this.

The storm victims on the boat could see their fellow men on dry land. They waved and couldn't understand why no one tried to help them. It seemed to them that the bonds of humanity had broken down. 'Why don't they throw us a line?'

they thought. Surely they could do so from those high cliffs. What seemed a long period of hopelessness passed, with no indication that the watching crowd were going to help or indeed act in any way – they just looked on, spectators of an unfolding tragedy. The danger had frozen all on board into inaction and almost acceptance of the worst, with no hope but to endure the dark, violent skies and the loud roar of the waves splashing and shaking every part of the stricken vessel. The crew and passengers must have been more or less resigned to their fate, when as a last desperate resort Guze Ruggier shouted out:

'I'll do it! I will swim across and take a line to the shore.'

Everyone gasped in disbelief. They wondered who this seaman was. Why had he volunteered? Perhaps it was rash belief in himself and his swimming ability. Perhaps he felt he knew the sea and its ways and trusted it more than he did the disintegrating ship. Or was it his innate Maltese trait to do his utmost to help others? He didn't stop to think that the attempt was against all odds but stepped forward and told the other crewmen to tie a long rope around his waist. Then he took off his shoes and sailor's cap and moved across to the lee of the boat. He had noticed that the bulk of the ship was taking the power out of the water, so that to this downwind side the resulting waves between the boat and the rocky shore were not as vicious as those further up or down the coast. Waves in a storm have an ugly, powerful and hostile look about them, but they also have a mathematically predictable rhythm that they keep to, which is altogether more calming. He looked at the waves, and he focused on this rhythm that he knew from experience gained in his youth and not on the loud periphery of wild spray. This gave him hope and courage. He made the sign of the cross, calling down God's protection as most Maltese would, and dived in to the swirling dark ocean.

Guze swam towards the shore. As he approached the rocks he felt the rhythm and waited for a suitable wave, then he swam faster to catch it. Only after a couple of tries was he able to catch a wave on the cusp, at the right time to propel him towards the rocks. The wave pushed him right up, then just as it was about to force him against the jagged rock face it lost its power and began to dissipate. It deposited him almost gently on the rocks, and he took the opportunity to grab hold of them with all his might. No sooner had the wave retreated below him than he began to scramble up, taking no heed of the gashes to his hands and feet. Twelve, thirteen, fourteen, fifteen seconds later, and he heard the 'woosch' of the next wave coming up below him and froze rigid, clinging again to the rocks lest the new wave dislodge him. Luckily, that next wave was smaller and it only sprayed his feet. He began to scramble higher, taking heed of the timing of the waves. Fourteen, fifteen … he froze again for a few seconds and then dragged himself up further. Twice more did this occur before he reached the top of the cliff and the safety of the dry shore. What a relief, and what an outcry from those he greeted on shore – but an even louder cry of exhilaration and hope from the people still on the boat, who had watched the ordeal with bated breath.

The lifeline to the ship was

,eventually secured by his now many enthusiastic helpers and a sort of boson's chair was rigged up. It allowed for the safe passage of thirty-one people, one by one, across those ugly seas. The ship, however, had been impacted too long and by too many waves, and sadly broke up before the remaining four hundred other passengers and crew could be brought to safety. The hope they had been given was in vain. The captain must have cursed himself for not taking the alternative westerly course he could have plotted, away out towards Ireland, after he had rounded that most north-west tip of Wales. He should have stayed on the starboard tack, but had been seduced by the shorter, riskier eastern route that would have brought him to his destination and fortune quicker. The basic sailor's rule, 'If it's rough you are safer out at sea, not close in shore', would now have haunted him. Who would have thought that plotting a course to Ireland, of all places, would have been the right one, instead of the one closer to home? He had thrown his caution, and indeed his fortune, to the wind in more ways than one. A monumental British maritime tragedy had occurred.

It wasn't so much the gold medal he was given that made Guze famous for his deed. It was more that, soon after the shipwreck, Charles Dickens wrote about it in his widely read book *The Uncommercial Traveller*, in Chapter 2, entitled 'The Shipwreck'. Guze would from then on be marked out, no matter what ship he was on. People would say, 'Look, that's Joe who saved the people on the *Royal Charter*.' Guze's story left James spellbound. It fired his imagination and made its mark on his mind and in his heart. The people of his small island were as brave as any in the world. This proved it – and so would he.

Focusing again down from that magnificent Valletta vantage point, James could see across on the other side of the harbour Fort St Elmo, which guarded the city of Birgu behind it. The other two cities, Senglea on the right and Cospicua further to the left, were also visible, with their massive high-walled turreted fortifications guarding the closely packed, flat-roofed limestone houses and the many church domes and steeples. This magnificent harbour, a welcoming site to any ship passing through the sometimes stormy

Mediterranean, offered immediate safety to friends. The high bastion wall and fortifications, on the other hand, were a threat to any enemy wanting to use it. This had been the case for hundreds of years, and it was still the same now. Looking back at the ships, James wondered which propulsion system they used most and in what conditions: the power of the *Royal Charter*'s steam-driven propeller was clearly not enough in that desperate situation, and its sails had been uncontrollable and redundant. These and many other unanswered questions he was keeping for his father's return.

Now for the second time James saw the new India mail steamship, which also had three masts and one funnel. It had all the latest equipment: he had been told about the details by an English sailor down in the harbour only the week before. These ships had been specially built for quick passage through the Suez Canal, but not all the ships were bound for trade with India and the Far East. It was not long ago that transport ships carrying the wounded from the Crimean War had anchored here. Those who were too sick to travel back to Britain had recuperated in the Malta Bighi hospital before being transported home. Warships, trading ships and passenger ships sailed in and out, but the largest ships flew the Union Jack, as Britain had officially administered Malta for nearly fifty-five years now. Ship-spotting with a bit of imagination was almost as good as an adventure.

Ships and sails had become a large part of James's life, ever since his father had helped him get a job at a local sailmaking factory. It was run by an Englishman, Mr Smith.[2] Here James began to learn the skills of sailmaking, from the age of probably seven and until he was about fifteen. One day near the beginning of his apprentice time, the sail factory got an order to replace a torn jib of one of the larger two-masters. They had to make a new one and a spare back-up.

'You have to know your cloth – feel it, its thickness and its softness. Always know the line of the fibres. In a sail like this, always cut on the cross, parallel to the line of the main fibres, so that the cloth will naturally stretch in that line and this gives you the curve in the sail. Everything depends on the cut of the sail,' his boss, the master sailmaker, told him. 'It's all about accurate lengths, exact angles and strong and smooth stitching.'

Each width of cloth had to fit exactly into the next; the horizontal stitching line made the width of the cloth into the length of the sail. The sail had to let the wind give it a natural curve. The Maltese cloth from local cotton tended to be thicker and stronger then the Egyptian cotton cloth. They had both: it was a matter of price. The Egyptian was slowly becoming more popular.

'If you cut it wrong you waste the cloth, as it has to be done again.' The apprentice heard 'always', 'everything', 'must', 'straightaway', many times over.

The boss worked quickly, particularly on this job as it had a tight deadline: the ship had to leave port with its cargo in two days' time. James did his best to keep up, running around the large flat cutting tables, carrying thread, needles, scissors, darting here and there, doing as he was directed.

'This is the spine line – hold it down while I cut.'

He climbed onto the table to

make sure the sail was held with the right tension for the cutting process. The master sailmaker did the work and gave the orders; for the apprentice, the most important part was the cutting of the cloth. The last task done the previous evening had been to measure the old torn and tattered sail, which wasn't easy because of the state it was in. The master had written all the details down in his specifications log, calling out the measurements as he went along.

'Okay, let's see this cut.' Cutting with scissors was an art and it required the concentration that came from experience to make a lot of smaller snips into one true line. Looking at his piece of paper, he called out, 'Fifteen foot long and a top angle of 35 degrees of the jib.'

'Excuse me,' James said suddenly. 'You said fifteen and 35 degrees.'

'That's right, I did.'

'It was sixteen and 25 degrees – I heard it yesterday when you called it from the measuring rod and the compass.'

The boss scowled. 'Rubbish, lad. I wrote it down myself – here, look.' He showed James the piece of paper. 'You see?'

James stared at the piece of paper without comprehension.

'What the heck am I showing this to you for! You can't even read.'

'No, sir,' James said. 'But that doesn't matter. It was still sixteen and 25 degrees. You just wrote it wrong, that's all.'

'Don't be daft – 25 degrees at the top would make that a storm jib, and a pretty small one at that, but 35 is the norm. Except for the Genoa, which is wider, of course. Can't you understand? For God's sake, lad, we need to get this job done …'

He was about to turn back to his interrupted work when he straightened up.

'Very well,' he said. 'We'll check it again.' They went next door, got out the old sail and painstakingly re-measured it.

'Sixteen and 25 degrees it is,' he said, shaking his head.

Back in the cutting room Mr Smith bent over his paperwork and made the correction. As he wrote, a frown came over his face. He slowly straightened up again, lifted his face and raised his eyebrows.

'How did you do that?'

'What?'

'Remember those numbers out of all the numbers, and know there was a mistake. How did you do it?'

James shrugged his shoulders. 'I don't know. It just came to me. It's just something I can do.'

There was a silence in which Mr Smith noted that there was more to this lad than met the eye. 'Shame you don't read and write,' he said.

James knew he had done something out of the ordinary, and he bit his lip at the thought of not being able to read numbers. He felt it was his basic right to be taught, but he hadn't been. There were no schools. His small, precise hands were good at the tight stitching, and he knew that he was good at his job and had security there, but he was starting to find it boring.

His skill with languages was the key. He knew how to communicate and thus how to find things out. He could speak Maltese from his mother, Italian from his father and now English from his work. One day when he had wanted to know about the new India mail steamship, he had gone up to the hill known by the navy as *Nix Mangiare* ('nothing to eat') near the fish market. It was where boys and young men went looking for work, or begging for food or pennies, near the approach to the main Victoria Gates of the city of Valletta. There he spoke to an English navy officer he saw by the shore. He was not as shy as his friends were in approaching an Englishman, and if he'd any thought that he was likely to get brushed off, he was wrong.

'Good morning, sir,' he said. 'Fine morning.'

'Hello, son. Yes, it is nice and sunny today,' replied the officer.

Pointing at the new ship, the boy remarked, 'That's a strange ship over there. If that funnel was any bigger they could use it as a sail!'

The navy officer and James burst into laughter simultaneously. By coincidence, the officer was pushing to get more technology into the navy's ships and that funnel was indeed ridiculously large, so the joke struck a chord. They fell into conversation, and the officer explained in detail about the steam turbines that were the 'latest thing' fitted on ships, and how they drove dynamos, and how these in turn made electricity and light for the ship. James went home happy that he had got so much information, and knowing that most of it couldn't be found in books even if he had been able to read.

It was his usual way of finding things out. He would look at a person's face, talk to that person in his or her own language and make a joke: this opened the person up and allowed James to ask all the questions he wanted. It always worked. He used to remember the information he was given, together with an image of the person's face, as a sort of reference. He found he could remember almost anything that way. 'Who needs to read to find out about something?' he thought to himself. He did it his way, and would in time perfect and stubbornly stick to this 'information retrieval system'.

Although schooling had not given him rules and structures to learn things by, he found that at different stages in his life he occupied himself with learning particular topics. In his quest to speak languages, he found that there were certain areas about which it was important to be able to talk: in addition to exchanging greetings, you needed to be able to discuss food, travel, family and trade (which included money and counting). He always wondered how they learned these things in school and was more and more determined to perfect his own way and bring order to his dyslexic muddle.

At this time he began to develop his own counting system, which circumvented the blocks he had in his mind. As he couldn't read numbers he used a system of lines with a cross through every fifth one. This way his number could be read to the left or to the right, upside down or in any position: it still gave the number. His dyslexic mind used to read normal numbers jumbled around, so that 2 would seem upside down and more like a 7 – just confusing. He slowly grew his system, adding hieroglyphs as necessary, and became confident in its use.

He spent much of his time, when he was not working at the sail factory, playing with his friends. He noticed that his skin was fairer then some of theirs, probably because of his Italian or Sicilian ancestry. One of his best friends had a rather darker complexion, and in the height of summer, when they had been in the sun and done a lot of swimming, his skin turned almost black, perhaps reflecting his North African origins. But it wasn't an issue. They were all Maltese. People James knew had surnames like Hassan, Buhagiar, La Rosa, Portughese, Portelli, Stricktland, Borg: these names were found in places from North Africa to northern Europe, and reflected the time when Malta was ruled by the Knights Hospitaller.

Now in his early teens, James began to take note of and be influenced by the wider society he lived in, and his job give him opportunities to interact with many different people and organisations. He began to realise the power of languages and wondered how so many came to be spoken in his country. As ever, his perceptions became a part of his sharp memory.

4 Language wars and society blocks

'James, I've got a special assignment for you,' Mr Smith said. 'Please take these samples of cloth to the Baronessa de Piro. She wants to choose material for a sunshade. You know where the palace is?'

'Yes, by the main square in town,' James replied.

'The weave from the local cotton is better than the Egyptian stuff, but of course it's more expensive. See which one she likes.' Mr Smith was giving James more responsibility, and this was also one of his new ideas to broaden the market and not only make sails for ships.

James, wearing his best clothes, looked up at the huge entrance door. It was a hot summer's day and he would be glad to get inside out of the scorching sun. He had often wondered what was inside the nobility's palaces. The building was well placed, looking onto the main square in Valletta and adjacent to the Grand Master's Palace, which was now the seat of the British government. The complex entrance had a series of three 'doors': first, an ornate black wrought iron gate, only about 80 centimetres high, then the main large red wooden door, over three times James's height, and finally a glass *antiporta*, or inner door, with lace curtains.

The low wrought iron gate, with its intricate flower patterns, seemed a bit ridiculous, but it wasn't supposed to keep anyone out -- or rather it was only to keep the goats from coming into the front porch and dirtying it. These were a herd of about ten scrawny animals, all with bloated udders, that provided milk. Twice a week the maid would hear the tinkle of bells, and the calling shout of the shepherd, usually before ten in the morning. She would bring out tin bowls for the herdsman, who would squat down and milk the goats there and then in the street, the maid, in her clean white pinafore and white headscarf keeping behind the closed gate. She would pay the usual amount for the milk, smile and asked how his family were. He would gesture with his hands, return the smile and reply in his half-hoarse voice. After the goats were safely down the road, the maid would open the gate again and it would remain open for the rest of the day.

The next, much larger door was rather magnificent. It was elaborately panelled, with shining brass door knockers on each side. Two palm trees stood to left and right just inside the door, which was kept open during the day and usually only closed when the family were away. It would also be closed if there was a death in the family, when it would be draped with a black stripe. In this way it acted as a kind of message board. The last barrier, a closed glass white-framed door, was decorated with white lace curtains.

James pulled the shining bronze bell handle. He heard it tinkle and then, further away, a dog gave out a pedigree growl of warning. As he waited he caught glimpses through the glass door of the well-lit hallway inside. An elderly gentleman smartly dressed as a butler, with a rather noble and serious demeanour, came to the door.

'I was sent by *Sur* Smith of the sailmaking factory and I have these samples to show to the Baronessa,' James said.

After being ushered into the large oak-panelled hallway, James was led up one of a pair of a winding staircases, with marble steps and elaborately patterned dark wrought iron railings, which went up on either side: the luxury of a choice of stairs! At the top was a glass case containing stone and pottery ornaments, including one of a naked fat lady, the stone-age goddess of Malta. Some of the ladies today were almost as fat, thought James, but they certainly were not goddesses.

'What on earth were those ancient inhabitants thinking of, worshipping that,' he wondered.

Next he passed two large Roman-looking brown clay urns which could be touched as you walked by.

'Maybe they were from St Paul's ship when he became stranded on the island', his vivid imagination surmised.

An antique, half-broken block of sandstone with letters carved in it was the next exhibit, displayed on a stand a little further down the hall. The lettering was in a strange Arabic script and spelt out '*akbar*'; no doubt on the missing part of stone had been '*Alah*', the Maltese word for God. It was one of the few artefacts remaining from the Arabs' 200-year occupation of Malta, although the unwritten language would remain, being handed on by word of mouth from generation to generation. It was eventually written down using the Italian script and alphabet, and much later (1924) in its own new indigenous alphabet, which was tailored to express the Arabic guttural sounds that the Italian alphabet was unable to express.

The walls were filled with old golden-framed family portraits and shining swords, pistols and other weapons. Clocks of all shapes and sizes could be seen and heard everywhere. One picture of what looked like a Turkish sultan with an ornate two-feathered turban headdress studded with jewels, in a golden frame embossed with Islamic half-moons, probably represented Suleiman the Magnificent, the Turkish leader who was defeated in the great siege of 1565. The family could have acquired the portrait as bounty when the Turks left in a hurry and without time to dismantle their belongings, or it might have been part of the loot of a corsair's ship, previously stolen from a Turkish galleon. In any case, there was no way that it had been commissioned by anyone who lived on Malta. This picture was more a proud trophy for the victor than a show of tolerance of different nationalities.

There was also the usual shiny metal suit of seventeenth-century armour, and an elaborate helmet with a pointed front visor and little slats for the eyes that seemed to looked down at James as he walked past it. The boy instinctively increased his distance. This was a show that only the higher ranks of the military or the nobility, (in those days one and the same), would and could put on.

Other noticeable links to the past included the distinctly French furniture: an ornate mahogany *secrétaire à abattant* with a marble top, a Louis Quinze set of sofa and chairs in creamy pastel colours with asymmetrical shapes and curves of gold, and several more rococo mid-eighteenth-century pieces. Again, these were probably acquired from the French knights who left Malta in a hurry after Napoleon's takeover in 1798. Many of the knights who were expelled from the island were also to a considerable amount debtors of the inhabitants. None of these liabilities could be recovered from the knights, who were driven homeless and penniless from the island. The furniture, which was probably a bargain at the time it was acquired by the locals, was some of Europe's finest.

These decorations and furniture were a history lesson for James, although he was only superficially aware of the various influences of the different historical periods on the island and its inhabitants. Everything in the palace certainly conveyed the impression that this noble family had been here since early history, were still here now and would remain so. Furniture of this kind was to be shown off more than to be used, but all together it was part of the country's history.

Also in the hallway, along with shelves of old books, was a large novelty bureau, which when opened up turned into an altar with candlesticks and statues as required. This was used for private celebration of the Mass within the palace, a privilege which was another manifestation of the close ties between Church and nobility. After the priest had said Mass the altar would be closed up and revert to being a cupboard.

The first-floor landing had large

arched windows which looked down into a peaceful courtyard where there was a huge bougainvillea in full scarlet flower, together with lemon trees laden with large yellow fruits and a pond, no doubt full of goldfish, with a fountain in the centre. The sound of the trickling water gave a feeling of coolness and calmness on that hot day. The butler told James to be seated and wait, and he went on ahead through a large door. James felt special as the chair he sat on was higher than a usual chair and was a bit like a throne. It had smooth shiny wooden carved arms, and its tall padded back was embroidered with a crest (the lemon trees outside looked not unlike the picture in the crest – perhaps the family's old source of wealth, property and plantations). After several long minutes the butler returned and James was ushered through another high double door.

Adelaide de Piro was seated at the end of the large well-decorated room. She was nobility by birth, daughter of the fifth Marquis Cassar Desain, as well as wife to Marquis Francesco Xaverio, the fifth Marquis de Piro. Tapestries hung from the walls of the high silent room. A large fireplace with an elaborate mantel and dark marble surround dominated the main wall opposite the windows. The lighting was subdued, except for a bright bar of sunlight that slipped in through the louvred shutters on one side and highlighted a shimmer of dust. She was sitting, straight-backed, in a large, upright, uncomfortable-looking but nevertheless imposing chair, with a well-groomed chihuahua at her side, its crossed front paws and half-open eyes indicating that it belonged where it was. The lady's hands were folded in her lap in a sort of a set-piece pose. Her black silk dress was arranged in straight folds that reached her footstool. Trimmings of black Maltese lace around the collar and cuffs gave it a finer texture, as did her delicate jewels. Her face was beautiful, with smooth white skin. It was felt at the time that faces, even in private, should show calm assurance, good manners and above all total control. She did, however, greet the fourteen-year-old with a kind smile, which seemed to change the whole atmosphere.

'*Bon Giorno*,' she said – not the more usual '*Bongu*' (pronounced *bon jour*, a relic from the French times). It was more a test then a greeting.

James replied, '*Bon Giorno, Baronessa*' (as instructed by Mr Smith). Had he replied in Maltese '*L-fhodwa t-tajba*' (which is Arabic-derived), he would have failed her little game.

The basic rule was that French idioms, or French-Maltese, would have been totally frowned upon; the nobility had, at that time, an animosity towards any French influence, and not without reason. There was also another subtle reason for using the Italian greeting rather than the Maltese. The aristocracy needed to differentiate their position and establish the 'level' of the meeting. The French use *vous* instead of the colloquial *tu*, the Germans *Sie* instead of the more familiar *du*, and the Italians *lei* instead of *tu*. You can't, however, differentiate your familiarity in Maltese: the words don't exist. This is, on the other hand, an advantage for the Maltese in that their greeting is more friendly, or egalitarian, as in a small community there is less need to establish social levels; people automatically belong to the 'the Maltese family'. However, it carries a danger in that outsiders, who perhaps do not have your interests at heart, are greeted in the same way and are perhaps thus more readily accepted. A response from James in Maltese (Arabic) would have shown that he had little appreciation for society's hierarchy. This response would have triggered a mental appraisal and any disdain would not show: there would be no outward sign or facial expression of this inner complexity. Had he answered in English 'Good morning, your ladyship', it would have been clever, but not yet appropriate, although the present generation had taken to calling their children by English forenames rather than the traditional Italian ones – so complex was the linguistic social environment in Malta at the time. But James was up to it: he could have played it any way, and had an instinct for which of these cultural nuances was appropriate.

The discussion continued in Italian, and James answered politely as best he could. He proceeded to hand over the cloth samples and give some information about the local origin of the cotton, and how it was made and who wove it. A short description and comparison of the thickness and quality of the two samples was also given. The Baronessa wanted a light sunshade for her garden patio, so she could sit out on those hot summer days. On concluding the short business, he was thanked and offered a sweet from a small silver bowl, which he gladly accepted. As he left the magnificent room, he couldn't help feeling that he had been in the presence of royalty; gold and silver were the colours that flashed through his head as he walked out. It was not unlike the feeling he sometimes had when sitting in one of the great gilded baroque churches, such as St John's Cathedral in Valletta: all that art, gold and wealth. It was somehow comforting, and mixed in there was a little bit of pride. James was proud of himself for having spoken Italian. Yes, he was different. Yes, he could communicate to the nobility in 'their' language. Perhaps he could be a part of that set. A plethora of images flashed through his creative mind, fed by the environment he had just experienced. Then other images crept in, less encouraging: the dyslexia business, exasperation, and an emptiness that signalled unobtainability. He breathed a deep sigh. There must be a way forward for him to fulfil his own ambitions. He would not be resigned to the rut he perceived himself to be in. He would find a way round his difficulties.

On his walk home four images continued to flash up in his mind: an image of the palace he had just seen, an image of a bright large baroque church, an image of the British Governor's offices and then an image of his own humble home. It occurred to him that these images made up a picture of his island's society and the four main players in it: the nobility, the Church, the British and the poor Maltese. Could he move from one group to another? Would he always live on the cusp of poverty? Where did his future lie? If not with the nobility, then with the British? He asked himself these questions. There were people who got closer to the nobility and the government and advised them and worked for them. They were also well off. That must be a goal of his, to move into those higher circles. The words he had heard at work several times came thundering back to him: 'If you can't read or write, forget those higher jobs'; and the comment, 'You're a labourer and that is where you belong.' However, he believed there was something better.

These images suddenly cleared from his mind as just then he saw his friend Lely. They wandered down the steps towards the Customs House by the harbour sea front, chatting together. An elderly English sailor was just stepping off a taxi djhasa boat with his heavy kitbag.

'Sir, can I help you carry that?' asked James.

'That's kind of you. Please take it to the Hotel Empire right up at the top of the stairs.'

Both boys helped to carry the baggage, and the officer handed James a generous tip.

Walking up the hill, Lely complained, 'Why do you always get the tips while I getting nothing?'

'Don't worry – we will share it, of course,' James replied. 'But you should learn some English, you know. That is how you get the real money'.

Lely grimaced and screwed up his eyes – annoyed, perhaps even angered. Mentally, he chose to stick with what he knew and ignore the truth of economic reality.

*****

James's imaginings only reflected the surface of the island's reality. Taking a closer general look at the nobility, they were indeed a force throughout Malta's history. However, in James Martin's time there were a lot of disputes among them and they were rapidly losing their esteem. There was consequently a lot of discussion about who exactly were the nobility. The debate had been brought to a head because the nobility felt hard done by when, during a recent visit to Malta by the Prince of Wales, protocol gave members of the Chamber of Commerce precedence over the nobility. Their pride was hurt; they didn't feel that the British administrators were giving them due consideration. So in a joint written complaint, penned by Adelaide's father to Queen Victoria herself, they expressed their disgust. Thus on the prompting of the Queen, the British Administration set up a commission to decide who was indeed nobility in Malta. The Royal Commission was led by two judges, Dr S. Naudi and Dr Filippo

Pullicino, a member of the Council of Government between 1860 and 1869. It was realised that the British, in taking over the administration of Malta in 1815, had agreed 'to respect the ancient rights of the Maltese people'; so the acceptance of the Maltese nobility was argued to be part of the agreement. However, different people claimed the same title: some were nobility *de facto if* not *de jure.* This Royal Commission had to decide who were the rightful heirs, and kick the '*de factos*' out.

Nobility was often about obtaining recognition and about keeping lineage and retaining wealth and prosperity. The Royal Commission of Dr Naudi and Dr Pullicino determined various lines or origins of nobility. The older ones came from the times of Count Roger of Normandy, and these tended to hold the larger areas of property. The Inguanez family were among them, and dated back to 1350. Another category was set up in the times of the Knights Hospitaller, between 1530 and 1798. The de Piro family's nobility was granted in 1742 by Philip V King of Spain. If at that time you served the Knights well – and the de Piros had done so for probably over a century – or came into wealth (in the sixteenth century this was often achieved by becoming a corsair and plundering the treasures of other ships – in the name of the Knights, of course), in order to retain that wealth and give it permanence a hereditary nobility title was just what was needed. The different titles had different rules as to their inheritance and the different fees to be paid to various European kings, and keeping up with these and interpreting them was a major task. Nobility was, however, about retaining the official linage and privileges; it was also about being an important mediator between the Maltese people and the outside world or its administrators.

In the end, the Royal Commission allowed thirty-two of the titles, and from that day in 1877 the Maltese nobility were accepted on an equal ranking with other European nobility, as signed and sealed by Queen Victoria herself. No one could argue with that. A framed certificate was hung in the hallway of the Baronessa's residence, which the family were truly proud of. The commission also recognised a 'committee of Privileges', which was a group of the nobility who ruled over the disputes among them and also determined the line of heritage of the different titles. The Maltese nobility were now recognised and could mix with the rest of the nobility of Europe, and they would be invited to the relevant garden parties in future; and, more importantly, they would get to meet visiting dignitaries before those 'vulgar' local Chamber of Commerce people.

'Our, society in Malta is like a glass of whisky and water,' it was said. 'If we have no whisky, life is bland as water and goes nowhere; if we add a reasonable tot, it mixes and provides taste and life, and we prosper. However, if we add too much or add the wrong stuff, it will be our and our country's demise.'

Thus they understood it, and actively fostered outside contact and influence. They had to bring in the best whisky and mix it in the right proportions. It was part of their genetic sense as well. Being a small island with a limited population (about 120,000 in those days), Malta needed this outside stimulus. It was in those times of history when the people fell back on their own traditions and language and cut themselves off that they became weaker and poorer as a whole.

A small island in the middle of a busy sea that has a good harbour, an attraction to friends and foes alike, continually runs the risk of being overrun by superior foreign forces. The defence or strategy needed to counteract this risk was essentially the responsibility of the Maltese nobility. If the Maltese were to fight a more powerful enemy, they would – because of their limited resources – no doubt lose, with the resulting detriment to their people. So a task of the nobility was to guarantee the best 'administrator for the Island'. Historical hindsight shows that they seem to have made the right decisions. The list runs from St Paul, to Count Roger of Normandy, to the Knights and then to the British: mostly good choices made for their times, insofar as the Maltese were able to influence things. However, this cosy order of nobility, church and poorer people had gone on for too long – as was realised elsewhere by the French with their revolution. And it did, at one time, all come to an end.

Napoleon was first and foremost a revolutionary. He came to power understanding that his authority was based on freeing the people from their corrupt aristocracy: 'Liberté, égalité, fraternité'. This must have been foremost in his mind as his galleons sailed into the Grand Harbour in 1798. The Grand Master von Hompech (German-speaking) had all but capitulated. He said that his charter did not include fighting other Christian brothers, only infidels. The Knights, however, were a less cohesive and rather corrupt group at that time, and the Grand Master's decision effectively brought an end to the Knights' reign in Malta.

The Knights, who had ruled Malta for 280 years, historically had a strict code of conduct and came from the best European families. They belonged to *langues*, corresponding to their areas of origin. Each *langue* lived in its own *auberge*, or palace. When the Knights arrived in 1530, they comprised eight *langues*, appropriately represented by the eight points of the Maltese cross, their symbol. These were Provence (part of modern France), France, Auvergne (another part of modern France), Italy, Aragon (part of modern Spain), Allemagne (modern Germany), England and Castille (Portugal). So the languages of all these different places would have been heard in the streets of Valletta. Mostly Italian was spoken, with French ever trying to push through. Spanish would have been quite economically powerful and worth a few extra payouts to the Maltese (the Spanish kings were well represented), as also was Portuguese. German and English books were hardly stocked in the libraries, and English in particular, with its many strange pronunciations and dialects, would have been a marginal language not holding much noble kudos. Like Maltese, it couldn't differentiate between the familiar (*du*) and the reserved (*Sie*), which was particularly important to the noble Knights, so it was hardly a European language of cultural note.

It was an honour and a privilege for a family to have one of its sons in the order of the Knights Hospitaller. 'They would pledge the purity of their line, and his noble blood would bring grace and honour to the Order. They pledged that they would die for the glory of Christ.' The selection process of the Knights was vigorous and the order was able to choose only the best. They were a powerful band of independent fighters, and did not have to answer directly to any one country. They fought for the Church and the Pope, but tended to have their own agenda. The chosen sons, however, did not always look on this privilege as a blessing, not least because they had to take a vow of chastity and were supposed to be celibate.

A celibate fighting knight is, of course, more a myth than a reality. Examination of one of the Grand Master's expense records, which have recently come to light, show that he had a stone spiral staircase (a *garigor*) built directly from his palace bedroom to the laundry maid's room below (presumably so that he would always have clean laundry and so that not everyone would get to see his dirty washing). Among expense items attributed to 'Angelica' (the beautiful young laundry maid) were, for some reason, expensive furniture, dresses, cloaks and jewellery. In all, the illegitimate offspring of the Knights were so plentiful that some of the obvious ones were given the name 'belonging to the Hospitallers' or '*Tal Spiteri*', which has survived today as a common Maltese surname. Noble European DNA was thus to be found in many families, of all classes, in Malta, although it certainly was not recognised as such. A noble lady's butler probably had as much European 'blue blood' as she did. Malta was a melting pot in every sense of the word.

Over the years of the Knights' reign, the French members were the most numerous and contributed most to the Order in Malta. They occupied the largest palace, the Auberge de Castille, but in spite of the French dominance they were unable to establish their language to any great depth. The chosen official common language of the Knights remained Italian (in fact, Tuscan Italian) although many military maps, plans and documents were still in French.

With the arrival of Napoleon, everything changed for the Knights of the French langue. They belonged to the French aristocracy, and derived their money from their families back home; but Napoleon was one of their own, so to speak – so this presented a major dilemma. The French Knights, taking no risks and knowing Napoleon's reputation, were in fact the first to vacate Valletta, and well over half of them headed back home to France instead of joining up with the invading French victors. He had too much of a reputation and too many enemies among the French aristocracy. Napoleon knew that Malta was, like France, ruled by an aristocracy: the Knights and the Maltese aristocracy as well. He believed that the common people of Malta were ripe for revolution. He was particularly incensed by the fact that the rulers of Malta still kept slaves: these people needed to be free. The common masses must have been jubilant when he immediately threw out the nobility and didn't recognise their rights at all. They were also glad, at this stage, to be rid of the Knights. Slavery was abolished and many slaves got their freedom for nothing, staying on in Malta as ordinary citizens.

Knowing that the protection of

knowledge and gaining it was the nobility's means of maintaining power, Napoleon promptly disbanded the university and its structure. He was right here, because even though Malta had a renowned university it was only the nobility and their learned associates who were able to enter its doors. So he turned the university into a central college for all, an '*école central*', and introduced new educational policies. First, all private schools were shut down; and later, he went on to establish primary and adult education.

All the pieces for a bloodless revolution were in place. The Maltese poor would be a free, liberated people and would be able to learn and grow and establish their freedom. Napoleon would go down in Maltese history: never had a revolution been so easy. The capitulation agreement with the French was signed on the French side by Commander Boisredont de Ransijat and on the Maltese side by Baron Mario Testaferrata, Dr G. Nicholas Muscat, Dr Benedict Schembri, Councillor V. F. Bonnani and the Bailiff of Turin Frisari. With this, the French language at last began to acquire ascendancy over Italian.

But there was a problem. Napoleon, or rather his administrators, had added another vision to the basic three of his revolution. It was now 'Liberté, égalité, fraternité … et avidité': greed. A further miscalculation was that Napoleon did not understand the 'hot wire' that existed between the minds of the poor and the Church. He abolished the dreaded inquisition and believed that this would win over the populace, but it didn't. The Church played an important part in the Maltese way of life. It had many traditions and contributed to people's daily lives through its work in the parishes and in their homes: it was the welfare system for the poor. Backed by the inquisitor's terror, it also guarded society's moral issues. The people were hardly allowed to make up their own minds about anything. Disrespecting the Church, which he claimed to be in league with the nobility, Napoleon went on, it is said, to plunder its buildings, removing the large silver candlesticks and other treasures which the Maltese had appreciated every time they saw them. The splendour of the churches broke the monotony of their simple homes. This robbery was thus perceived to be against the people, not only against the Church, and may have lost Napoleon the support of many commoners and hence his revolutionary base.

However, perhaps the most vindictive action the French undertook was to hold some of the nobilities' children hostage and removed them to France. This hit hard in the very family-oriented society. The nobility were quick to seize on it and were instrumental in starting a counter-revolution aimed at getting rid of the French. This they did in a skilful manner. Although the first words of dissent were voiced by a priest, the nobility assisted in the process – one of their leaders being the Marquis de Piro, who lost his life probably as a result of the struggle. When the Maltese rebellion began to falter they called in the British, and none other than Nelson blockaded the harbour with his ships and forced the surrender of the French in 1800. Again the nobility had brokered the introduction of 'suitable' administrators for their island. The nobility had won that battle and were back in charge, but the Maltese majority, without knowing it, had lost the war by not securing their educational and developmental future and thus they remained shackled in poverty. The abolition of slavery, the removal of the inquisitor and the establishment of the Napoleonic legal code did, however, stand as Napoleon's lasting legacy.

Conventional history tells us that the Maltese counter-revolution began because the French stole the silver candlesticks from the churches. Some, however, believed that was not what sparked the uprising at all. Rather, it had been a well-orchestrated campaign against the French, the Maltese nobility colluding with the Church to raise anti-French sentiment among the populace so as to dupe the Maltese peasants into action –action which would in fact kill their chances of a fairer society and, importantly, education for all. No man in his right mind would fight to win silver candlesticks and thereby lose his family's future education and development and the chance to throw off the chains of poverty. Had the French remained and had their 'adult education concept' functioned, it could well have created a different educational climate that would have benefited the people fifty years later.

The implications of this for James could have been profound. But the school system that Napoleon set up, and that could possibly have helped him, had not endured and he would receive no help. Also, the rigid social classes remained, and he had little chance of progressing from one strata to another and perhaps moving out of poverty. The system was set to block him and others like him. In addition, his potential knowledge of French would now be restricted to a few words, though the Maltese language did take up and use the perhaps most important phrases in any language, *bongu* (good day), *bonswa (bon soir*, good night) and *portmoni* (money purse)! Adult schooling, available for all, would not be introduced in Malta for another fifty years after the French reforms were defeated. This unacceptably long delay was not so much because the British administrators (who took over from the French) didn't bother, but more because of indecision due to the unresolved conflict between the language fronts of Italian, English and Maltese. This fifty year delay, during the early 1800's also marked one of the worst periods of poverty, when many people had no jobs, little food and only the pavements to sleep on.

Paolo Pullicino, elder brother of Judge Filippo, was the Maltese credited with breaking this deadlock, becoming the eventual 'father of Maltese education'. He was a highly educated man, having gained a degree at the University of Malta, then attended the La Sapienza University in Rome and finally studied at the Sorbonne in Paris. It was probably the influence of the Sorbonne that ignited the French dream of 'Égalité des genres dans l'éducation et par l'éducation' in him, and education for all. It is interesting that it took the studies of an academic at the French seat of learning in Paris to establish the educational ideals of the revolution in Malta, rather than the dictate of Napoleon's conquering forces. Though an ordained priest, who became a Monsignor and a Canon, he was appointed by the British administration to be Minister of Education and pushed through these ideas. In 1850, Paolo Pullicino set up the first Scuola Serale, or evening school for adults, in Zabbar. This educational strategy appeared to be a joint effort between the Church and the British Administration, who shared a common goal of education: the Church educating in religion and the government in the English language. The first lessons began in arithmetic, reading and writing. Canon Pullicino, with his belief in education for all and his ability to communicate with both the British administrators, the Church and the Italian grouping, was well placed. He also used his Church connections to announce the benefits of these evening classes at Sunday services in all the parishes.

Paolo Pullicino was the first Maltese to encourage the masses to pursue education. P. J. Keenan, in his commission report of 1878 wrote:

> The achievement in the space of 30 years goes to the credit of one man, Pullicino. In the whole of my experience, at home and abroad, of men whose lives have been dedicated to education, I have not met, or heard of, any man who combined in so interesting a degree the qualities of incessant devotedness to duty and of an earnest and enthusiastic pursuit of his own

ideal of what is best. No man could review, as I have done, the official life of Dr Pullicino without entertaining an almost inexpressible admiration of his patient industry and of his enormous ability.[3]

The schools Paolo Pullicino set up grew, and in one form or another still exist today. As well as opening the schools, he set the curriculum and personally trained the teachers. Hence the English and the Maltese languages received more exposure under this new system

Many people in Malta had suffered disadvantage and oppression due to the lack of education, which had been so difficult to get started. It was a hot potato of high politics, which is still something of an issue today. Two cultural factions were working to win the minds of the people. On the one hand, there were the anti-reformists who promoted Italian: this was the traditional language of the elite and of civil society, or the network of dominant ideological and legal institutions that glued the fabric of society together and supported the existing hegemony (Administration/Church/nobility). On the other hand, there were the British administrators who obviously promoted English. There were also a growing number demanding more use and representation of the native language, Maltese. This Italian–English–Maltese conflict held up the establishment of an educational system aimed at the common man. The various authorities couldn't agree on the content of the education, so one blocked the other and it just didn't happen. The language debate was further complicated by the fact that the Church still wrote and spoke and held its religious services in Latin. There were also the indigenous Maltese, who had very little say at all: Maltese was, according to some administrators at the time, only 'a language fit for the kitchen'.

It was against this complex political background that Paolo Pullicino pushed through the establishment of the first common schools. He pacified the Italian lobby, gave the Church's needs their due, added English, and spoke to Maltese interests by also including their language, which was written with the Italian alphabet. The factions having been thus brought together, an educational support base could be established. This stage marked the beginning of the ascendancy of English to the detriment of Italian and eventually gave the Maltese the many advantages that this world language offered – more so than if Italian had been retained as the dominant tongue. It was also due to Paolo Pullicino that Maltese began to be used in a teaching context, as most courses had some basics in Maltese. This kick-started the beginning of Maltese as a seriously taught, written and read language that was used in education. The Maltese language also slowly began to replace Italian in the law courts and later in the ministries. Maltese would eventually, in 1924, change its alphabet from the Italian to its own, but the main thing was that people were being taught in the Maltese they understood.

Paolo Pullicino came from a family that had the pursuit of civic welfare ingrained in its values, eventually claiming 400 years of continuous civic duty. The author J. B. Cassar wrote: 'The family is the hallmark of tradition in public and national duty, upholding the sacred rights of their country in their capacity as representatives of the people'.[4] Pullicino could never have anticipated that his educational endeavours would result in one of his descendants becoming the first female representative of the Nationalist Party just three generations later. It was staunch, dependable people like this who, however slowly, were instrumental in setting up the educational infrastructure.

Although progress was made in education, health and wealth, the established structures were protected by those they served. A radical shift towards equality in the society's balance would not come until political democracy was established on top of this educational base. That would not be until nearly a century later. James Martin, however, didn't benefit from this educational and support structure. He had to sort out his mind and his life on his own. He could see no way through for himself if he stayed on Malta. He thus began to think of finding his fortune outside the island.

*****

It was said that there were two kinds of Maltese: those that stayed and those that left. At this time nearly 15 per cent of the population had emigrated over the previous half-century. It was also said that those who went abroad were either pushed or pulled. Most were pushed by the poverty and associated conditions in their limited homeland, which was often unable to provide for its by now 140,000 inhabitants. To say that James, perceiving the local environment as limiting, was pulled by the opportunities that the wider world offered would, however, not be the full story. There were many things that indicated to him that he should go, but also others that told him he should stay at home.

Among the positives of the island, he remembered with joy the traditions and festivities that gave him a sense of belonging. He worried that if he left he would lose these. Every Saturday afternoon and evening many people from the villages would walk up and down the main street in Valletta, and once the gas lamps were on it was possible to stay out in the flickering light until late. That was where everyone got news of what was happening. It was the place to meet girls from the neighbouring villages as well. Everyone just strolled up and down and had a good time. The fastest and latest carriages were to be seen. James had once or twice taken the horse-drawn omnibus home with about fifteen others – it used to run between the villages and Valletta – but walking, which he enjoyed, was the way he usually got about.

The feast day that occurred every year was also a great time in his village. The people would all be out on the streets to see the processions and the local band, and there was singing and folk dancing until late into the night. Everyone would dress up in their finest clothes: the gentlemen in their dark suits, the other menfolk in their best trousers and white shirts, and the ladies in their bright cotton garments. The other big annual event was the carnival in Valletta, when everyone went to watch the colourful floats. This time people dressed up in fancy costumes and there were many different bands to listen to. It was all great fun. If a young man hadn't found a girl before, then he surely would during the carnival. At times such as these the island seemed like one big happy family. The bright colours of the floats contrasted with the *faldettas* that some of the women wore: full-length black gowns with flat cardboard headpieces that were supposed to catch the wind and cool their faces. His older cousin had told him to avoid these women because they were spinsters, and the superstition was that they could put a spell on you. He had always crossed over to the other side of the road when he passed one of them, and would secretly point his covered first and fourth fingers at her and say a little rhyme to ward off the evil eye. If all this had happened while he was passing a cemetery, it was even more frightening. It seemed stupid to him now that he was growing up, and he just didn't believe in it anymore, but it had made him frightened at the time. It was good to see the *faldetta* ladies joining in the festivities on these occasions – it seemed that they were human after all.

These, then, were the good times. Other thoughts brought a heavy feeling to his heart. He had seen the increase in the number of people around the harbour cities of Senglea. People moved out because the area was too crowded and the drainage systems didn't work well; there wasn't enough water to waste on flushing the drains, especially in summer when it was the hottest. Sometimes the whole place stank to high heaven; Il-Marsa, being low-lying, was particularly bad. Complaints to the Administration never had any effect. This problem with the drains was the cause of several bouts of disease that killed large numbers of people. The smallpox outbreak in 1830 was still talked about, as was the cholera of 1837 when up to 3 per cent of the whole population had died. The last cholera outbreak had been not so long ago, in 1867. Everyone had been warned about the symptoms: a sudden onset of watery diarrhoea, stomach cramps, nausea and vomiting. There was only a 50 per cent chance of survival if you got the disease. James also knew the symptoms of smallpox: high fever, headaches and vomiting followed by a facial rash. The authorities insisted on being informed if anything like this occurred. Then it wasn't just the sick who were affected. The quarantine measures that were brought in stopped all trade and put people out of work. His own sailmaking company, it was said (although this was before his time), had had to lay people off when there was an outbreak of disease as fewer ships had come into port to get new sails and the business had gone into a decline.

The Crimean War (1853–6) had led to a massive increase in British expenditure in Malta, resulting in jobs for nearly everyone, but that was now over and in the last fifteen years about 15,000 people had left to seek a living elsewhere: that was roughly 12 per cent of the population. Food was again in short supply; children didn't get enough to eat and they tended to grow up stunted; this generation seemed to be even shorter than the last. It was no place to stay for the poor. Migration was a continuing trend, and by the end of the nineteenth century nearly 20 per cent of the Maltese population would be living around the shores of the Mediterranean, away from home.

Some progress was made, and the state of the economy was perceived differently by some. Major Whitworth Porter, a Royal Engineer, wrote in 1858:

The condition of Malta at the present moment, as compared with what it was fifty years since, marks well the beneficial effect of British domination;

whilst a thriving population, a crowded port, and an ever increasing mercantile traffic, are the satisfactory results to which England can point, in proof that she has maintained the trust upon her, with honour to herself, and benefit to all connected with her.

James was not, however, fully convinced of this relative prosperity. He, like many others, felt that he would be better off away from the island. Such decisions are much easier to make as a fifteen-year-old with no commitments or ties. The condition of his mind also played a part in his decision. The cultural and social environment of Malta had failed his youth in its most important need, to get to grips with the dyslexic gaps in his mind and link up the important mental pathways. He had heard that there was recently a big push for education for all by this Paolo Pullicino – it was even announced in the churches on Sundays – but somehow he felt it wasn't for him. The support and social back-up just were not there yet. So James Martin left because Malta didn't provide him with enough opportunities and the right challenges to fulfil his dreams. He felt blocked by the society.

Perhaps the definitive thing that moved James to leave his homeland was the realisation that he viewed and saw things in a different way compared to the people around him. His mind was a lonely place that he had to manage by himself. Hiding his dyslexia, he built up a steely stubbornness and resolute belief in his own capabilities, which he knew were different. He was not afraid to test these abilities in the wider world, and he was excited at the opportunity of leaving. He would find a better environment for himself. He would carry with him his Maltese cultural DNA, which would be severely tested in the years ahead, and he would, no doubt, miss his village life, his capital city and all the festivities and community reinforcements of life. He was proud of them all. But this was behind him as he walked up the shaking gangway onto his first ship as a seaman/sailmaker, he only had his skills and knowledge of languages – part of his cultural heritage – (Maltese contained the grammatical structure of Arabic, Italian and by now, some English, so was a good basis to instinctively pick up other languages). All he had was his complex and unstructured "special" mind to back him up.

5 The miracle

At the age of sixteen James Martin had been taken on by the skipper of a merchantman that was calling at Malta, and after a tearful farewell to his family, who showered him with warm clothing, gifts and good advice, he embarked on his first voyage. It could have been in this first ship he worked on as a seaman that someone shouted to him, 'Hey you, Jimmy, come here'; the name was repeated and stuck, quite quickly replacing the foreign-sounding 'Antonio'. It could have happened some other way, of course, but this was a common occurrence on English ships at the time. The change from 'Martini' to 'Martin' was more obvious. He was eager to fit in and become one of the crew, and he wasn't bothered by the name change as it helped him to get on. His talents were soon recognised, and as well as carrying out all the dreary chores assigned to a young newcomer to a ship he automatically made friends with the ship's tailor, who also cared for the sails, the ropes and the rigging. He soon became adept at handling sails, perfecting his knowledge of how to repair, sew and replace every bit of needy canvas, as was customary on a sailing vessel that had a limited crew and trades. All this was to serve him well in his future life.

He'd had no difficulty changing ship when he arrived in Liverpool at the end of his first engagement. He chose this time a ship bound for the United States, and later moved on to other ships so that he could fulfil his desire to sail the seas and see the world. He grew in years and strength, and developed into a hardy and confident seaman – a friendly and popular figure on board and on the wharves, and in seaman's haunts in the larger ports. He was now a deckhand aboard a three-mast barque that had sailed from Liverpool four weeks previously, bound for the Indian port of

Bombay. Although the summer months were long past, the weather had been kind in the Bay of Biscay and the wind in the Mediterranean was favourable. There had been a short stop at Gibraltar, and another at Malta for water and provisions. This last had been particularly welcome for Martin as he had been looking forward to returning to the island. He was thrilled as his vessel entered the Grand Harbour to be welcomed by the enveloping embrace of the towering bastions and battlements of Valletta on one side and the Three Cities on the other.

When he saw the Grand Harbour, childhood memories rushed back to him. As a boy he had known the many inlets and creeks around the island's coastline and had naturally come to love the sea: fishing, swimming and diving for sea urchins – it was all part of his life. He remembered how he had spent much of his time on the rocky shores of the two main harbours around Valletta, watching with awe as the large sailing vessels manoeuvred gracefully within those confined waters, backing sails, hauling them down, adapting sail area to the wind and to the particular task in hand. He studied the interplay of anchor and sail necessary for the vessel to reach a desired anchorage and the precautionary use of a whaler or two when the vessel was ungainly and did not readily respond to the rudder. He had been away from his old sailmaking job for what seemed a long time now, but he had often been told that the quality of the Maltese cloth was such that vessels came from far and wide specially to renew or replace their sails at Valletta. He always preferred to use Malta cloth to repair any sails. The sailcloth industry had grown over years, as had production of the prized variety of cotton that adapted itself so well to the island's poor soil. Many hundreds of workers in the cotton fields and in the weaving shops of Zebbug and Qormi made a living from the industry, although cheaper cotton from Egypt was increasingly being imported to the detriment of the local cotton farmers. These facts and memories were left behind him as the ship sailed out of the Grand Harbour again, but he wondered briefly whether he would ever return or whether this would be his last sight of Valletta.

The passage through the Suez Canal was slow and laborious, involving much towing from the shore and hauling by the ship's boats. The canal, although shortening the journey to the east, was not very practical for sailing vessels. Out of Port Suez, the ship took advantage of the strong winds, even as they rose to near gale force. The skipper used all the sail he could to get every advantage from the favourable run. Alas, he failed to temper his enthusiasm as the weather deteriorated, and he refused to heed the warnings spelt out by the shrieking of the rigging, by the protest of the creaking timbers, and by the repeated advice of older, more experienced hands. The skipper held on, just as a gambler holds on to a winning streak. He was foolish, especially as the light was poor. Then suddenly it happened. The mainmast, heavily over-canvassed, could take no more. Part of the rigging snapped just as the vessel was heeling hard to port with gunwales awash, and the top fifteen feet of the mast snapped off with a loud crack, flying overboard and dragging with it rigging, spars and shredded sailcloth. As the ship, relieved of her topsail, swung violently over on to the starboard beam, right into the trough of a rogue wave, the sea swept viciously across the deck. There was no hope for Martin the sailmaker, who at the time was attempting to reach the shelter of the wheelhouse. Caught unsecured in the open, he was swept into the turbulent waters of the Red Sea in full storm.

HMS *London* had just passed through the Suez Canal on her way to Zanzibar, making far better time than Martin's sailing ship. She had called at Malta for coaling and her next stop would be Aden. The captain had made the journey before and knew how vessels of various sizes and nationalities converged on the eastern end of the canal. Steaming through the night on that stormy sea, as a precaution he doubled the lookout watch both fore and aft and found that it gave him greater peace of mind, for many of the vessels he encountered were under sail and having a difficult time in the high wind and heavy sea.

This was the blurred shape that James thought he saw coming towards him in the early hours of dawn, the throbbing sound of its engines at first hardly noticeable but slowly turning into a full-sounding symphony in his ears. The closer it came, the wider awake he was. His hand stretched out as if clawing at the shape he saw, but when he tried to shout to gain attention, barely a croak came out. The ship was now up close, only 30 yards to the east, and he could see dim navigation lights. However, as soon as the ship was parallel to him he was plunged into darkness. The little light of dawn had been blocked off by the bulk of the vessel. No lights were reflected; he was in the ship's shadow, too close to it. It was night again, and no one could see him. The two minutes it took the boat to sail by seemed a lifetime. He struggled desperately, waving his hands and trying to shout, but still only a whimpering cry seemed to come, which couldn't be heard. He repeatedly called for divine intervention – not really a prayer, and he swore at the same time. As the stern of the boat passed, all hope seemed to come to an abrupt end. James's life was passing him by, out of his control.

The rays of the sun were then suddenly exposed again and like a theatre stage's spotlight beam highlighted those desperate hand-waves, which luckily caught the eye of the aft watchman. He felt sure he saw a spar with a man lashed to it drifting on the starboard side – a miraculous sighting. The speed with which the wreckage and the ship parted was, however, such that there was hardly sufficient time for the lookout to ascertain whether the human being he thought he had seen was a corpse or was definitely still alive. It was his risk; he could have kept quite, not being sure, and he was half asleep anyway.

'Man overboard at starboard aft,' he shouted at the top of his voice. It was a fortuitous decision indeed, which was heard and carried by the captain, who happened to be near the wheelhouse. He give the immediate order to slow down and go about. The young watchman then followed the recognised Man Overboard drill. He stood up on the first rung of the railing and kept an outstretched hand pointing at the object he had seen, so as not to lose sight in that rough grey dawn. The large ship swung around to enable the crew to have a closer look at the wreckage. No ordinary sailing ship would have managed the manoeuvre in that sea, but the three-master had the assistance of a steam engine which facilitated the tight turn.

Martin was only just aware that someone was pointing in his direction, and he saw a small boat being lowered down, but all too slowly. With rescue within reach, his mind slackened and the images in his head receded, his resolve weakened by the assumption that he had made it. He began to slip down and away. Then his face felt the sting of water, rather than the touch of the wind, and instinctively his breathing shut down. The rope around him began to unravel.

The tender with three men in it – one rowing, the others looking out – approached a large piece of drift wood, but it was empty. Another spar floating near it was also empty; no body was in sight. They turned, with outstretched arms, palms facing up, finger splayed, and looked back at the pointing watchman. He saw that they were doubting him but he nevertheless kept faith, vigorously stabbing his finger in their direction. One man took the boat hook and plunged it into the water under the spar, where he thought he saw a darker shadow. It struck resistance and as he pulled, dragging it up, a man's clawed hand broke the surface. The seaman with the hook, now excited, shouted out loud. The others turned to look towards him, slowly shaking their heads to indicate that all was lost. Two of them grabbed the deadweight and together heaved it into the rocking tender. One man slipped, falling back in the boat, and the body went crashing down against the boat's side. It suddenly spasmed, and then James jerked back to life, spluttering, croaking and vomiting out a projectile of salt water and slime. A desperate gasp for air, then coughing and retching, made the miracle complete. The faces of the three hardened seamen broke into broad smiles.

James could not, however, fathom out where he was but his aching body responded willingly to the comfort and warmth of the mattress and blankets in the ship's sickbay, the like of which he had not experienced in the cramped sleeping quarters and hammocks of the ships in which he had sailed. It was a whole day before his befogged mind could comprehend his extraordinary luck. He had not broken any bones and, although shaky, he was able to get back on his feet. The incident was duly noted in the ship's logbook. The next day the captain made the unusual decision to open a barrel of rum for all to celebrate. Jimmy Martin – barely able to take part, not being a drinker – nevertheless experienced the joy and remembered some of the gatherings he had been to back home. He was twenty-three years old, and he had his life ahead of him.

By the time HMS *London* reached the port of Aden, James was fit enough to be put ashore. Bidding farewell to his saviours and thanking them for the clothes they had given him, he went to a small and cheap seaman's hostel run by a Yemeni Arab. Inquiries revealed no news of Martin's stricken sailing vessel, and he assumed that she had foundered. Within a week he had signed up on a merchant steamer bound for Bombay, and after a short stay in that city, to which he took a dislike, he found an opportunity to join a smart American steamer bound for Zanzibar. Zanzibar had not previously entered his mind – it was an out-of-the-way place, its name conjuring up strange people and curious customs – but this move fitted in with his plan to serve on different kinds of vessels and travel the world. He might also be able to link up again with the blue-jackets of HMS *London*, who had saved him in the Red Sea.

Martin had not reckoned on the American skipper of the steamer being a drunkard and in every way an impossible person. He was burly, tough, and disciplinarian to the point of cruelty. The ship was sailing in ballast, but there was certainly no shortage of liquor on board and the captain was never sober throughout the voyage. He bawled out his orders, and cursed and swore without provocation at one and all. As the ship crossed the Indian Ocean he muttered unintelligibly to himself and seemed bent on some mischief, busy with his charts and his sextant. On the day before they were to reach land the captain's drinking increased. He set the vessel's course on a straight line pointed at the eastern coast of Zanzibar, made the helmsmen – among them James Martin – swear that none of them would alter the course of the ship in the slightest degree on pain of being severely punished, and retired to his cabin hugging a couple of bottles. He locked himself in, with orders that he should not in any circumstances be disturbed. It was not clear whether his plan was to wreck the boat and claim on insurance.

When danger arose and the presence of the skipper was needed, he was completely lost to the world. The coral reef, the shoals, the sandbanks all loomed suddenly out of the darkness. The charts were locked in with the captain, and the vessel charged on to the fatal destination that the captain had clearly planned for her. Martin was at the wheel. He did his utmost to slow down and save the ship, but with little effect. Flashes of panic came to his mind as he envisaged the horrors of his last encounter with the dark sea. Not again! He controlled his mind, his images and his panic with the self-discipline he had learned. Luckily it was low tide, and the ship merely ran aground on a sandy beach with a shattering bump. She was held fast at the prow and miraculously not badly damaged, and she stayed more or less upright; the problem was to get her afloat again.

This disaster had been witnessed by the crew of a Royal Navy cutter that was hiding up a narrow creek near by, screened by mangrove trees. The cutter, one of two in Zanzibar waters, was on anti-slave patrol, and had been on the lookout for the slave-laden dhows which continued the now illegal trade that the British government had resolved to suppress. The crew of the stricken American vessel put out stern anchors, and as the tide rose warped the ship with the help of the British blue-jackets. Slowly and with much effort the ship moved; the rising tide, twelve feet of it, was a powerful and irresistible lifting force. Before long the vessel could go astern and was towed in for damage inspection to Zanzibar Town, about fifty miles away on the western side of the island. Compared with the first rescue James had been involved in, this one was easily achieved.

6 Livingstone's base camp

If James Martin had initially thought that this small island he had arrived on was in any way like his own native island, the comforting idea would have quickly been dispelled. Malta was sometimes seen as a base for entry into North Africa and Egypt, and Zanzibar was similarly considered an island entry point to Eastern Africa, first used by Livingstone. The Africa they entered was, however, quite different.

The 1870s and 1880s brought about very important developments in East and Central Africa. The main causes were the opening in 1869 of de Lesseps's canal joining the Mediterranean to the Red Sea – the Suez Canal – and the ever increasing number of 'steamers': ships that relied on steam-driven propulsion instead of, or in addition to, sail. These novel facilities fired the imagination of shippers and skippers to open up new sea routes, and little-frequented ports like Suez and Aden grew in importance as stations for coaling and the replenishment of stores. Up until then the inhospitable and unfrequented coastal waters of East Africa, from Cape Guardafui to Mozambique, had held little attraction, except perhaps to the dhows that since time immemorial had sailed from the Persian Gulf to Zanzibar and back, relying on the prevailing monsoon winds to carry their miserable cargoes of slaves to Arabia, to India and to Persia. The early explorers of East and Central Africa – Livingstone, Speke, Burton, Grant and Baker – either travelled by sea via the west coast, round the Cape of Good Hope, or overland up the River Nile from Egypt and Khartoum. Now that the new route via Suez made the journey so much shorter, the importance of Zanzibar as a stepping-off port grew rapidly for an increasing number of European missionaries and explorers, mainly British and German, who were anxious to carry the Christian faith to pagans and to draw maps of unknown areas of the world. Great Britain, the leading maritime and naval power at the time, built up her influence in Zanzibar and the surrounding seas sufficiently to be able in 1873 to persuade the Sultan of Zanzibar, Seyyid Barghash bin Said, to prohibit if not slavery itself then the carriage of slaves by sea. This ban was enforced by a small fleet of Royal Navy cutters and whalers that patrolled the Indian Ocean off the east coast of Africa, particularly around Zanzibar and Pemba. The Royal Navy sailors had many a skirmish with slave traders on the high seas, but it was difficult for them to free the captives since the slavers disposed of their human cargo by jettisoning it into the sea whenever a naval patrol was sighted. The crews of the naval boats were based on Zanzibar, and on nearby Grave Island memorial stones to this day bear witness to the courage of those who died in performance of their duty. Stores and supplies, arms and ammunition, and replacement crews would be provided by a Royal Navy depot ship anchored in Zanzibar Harbour. HMS *London*, which snatched James Martin from certain death by drowning in the Red Sea in 1879, fulfilled such a mission.

Martin's first impression of Zanzibar was one of disappointment. In the second half of the nineteenth century, Zanzibar was in many ways anything but attractive. Visitors arriving found the scene on the foreshore cluttered with rubbish and with pariah dogs scavenging among the corpses of slaves who had dropped dead there or had been callously discarded by their owners. The Stone Town was a cramped collection of narrow streets, layers of wooden balconies, dirty walls, overhanging rusty tin roofs and closed doors everywhere; some of the latter, elaborately decorated with brass studs, hinted at the wealth that lay behind them. The air had a distinct smell that was both attractive and repulsive. The pleasant scent of tropical fruit, cloves, nutmeg, cardamom and other spices, and sometimes the whiff of fresh tropical rain, was all too often overpowered by the decaying stink of sweat and sewage, depending on the direction of the wind. It was an odour that stayed in the mind long after one had left the island.

Zanzibar was the gateway to the African mainland, which beckoned with dreams of spoils and riches but also the lure of inaccessible places. It was a land of life and death: in the first half of the nineteenth century, more than half the Europeans who ventured in – including Livingstone – died there of diseases such as malaria. Of those that returned from the mainland, some had gained instant fortunes in ivory, gold and black slaves. The myth and mystery of the unknown continent was kept alive by the many tales that were first told in Zanzibar.

Yet there were Europeans who fell under the spell of Zanzibar and, once there, did not want to leave. One such man was Sir John Kirk, who in 1858, aged twenty-six, joined the great missionary explorer David Livingstone as his doctor and botanist. When Kirk returned to the United Kingdom seven years later he was a tired and sick man, but as soon as he had recovered he sailed back to Zanzibar to work as a doctor and Vice-Consul, there to remain for over twenty years. He retired as British Agent and British Consul General, and a close and trusted friend of the Sultan, after having firmly established British predominance over the Sultanate. It would be ruled indirectly, as was the British custom.

Another Englishman to be caught by the island's spell was a young naval officer who first saw Zanzibar in 1874, when he was based there in connection with anti-slavery patrols. He was Lieutenant Lloyd William Mathews. Within three years he was inexorably drawn back to the place and volunteered to help the Sultan in training his military forces, without giving up his anti-slavery patrols. The young officer built up the Zanzibar army from 500 men to 1,300, and was then seconded to the service of the Sultan and subsequently made Commander of the Sultan's Forces. Five years later he was a Brigadier General and the Sultan's Chief Minister. Along with Sir John Kirk he pursued a relentless policy aimed at the suppression of slavery in East Africa. He led armed expeditions to the mainland to arrest Arab slave traders, to set up military posts under the Sultan's flag, and to sign treaties with various local African chiefs whereby they agreed to recognise the overlordship of the Sultan. Mathews's influence in Zanzibar and on the mainland of East Africa was said to exceed that of the Sultan himself.

Among Mathews's protégés and colleagues was James Martin, whom he had met in Zanzibar soon after the grounding of the American ship. Martin himself was to become deeply affected by the spell of Africa and would never again return either to his seafaring career or to his native island in the Mediterranean. The challenge of adventure would bind him inescapably to Africa. Zanzibar seemed so different to him. He saw Arab tradesmen dressed in their imposing headgear and gowns, some with ornate curved daggers attached to their belts. The women wore long black gowns that covered their heads, called *bui bui*, which looked a little the *faldettas* worn in Malta but were without the flatter headpieces. He found that he could pick out Arabic words and understand the gist of a conversation as the words sounded a lot like his native Maltese; indeed, he could count in Arabic. He could, by changing the accent of his Maltese, make himself understood by Arabs and carry on a basic conversation, which made the place seem less like a foreign land to him. Martin noticed that he could even understand some of the Swahili that was spoken by the locals. The native

Swahili greeting *jumbo, habari yako* included the word *habari*, which sounded like the Maltese *ahbariet*, meaning 'news': it meant 'hello, how is your news?' in Swahili – quite similar. He also quickly found that the Swahili numbers between six and nine were very similar to his own, and indeed to Arabic numbers as well. He worked out that if he wanted to discover a word in Swahili, he just had to ask an Arab who spoke Swahili, which he could do using his Arabic/Maltese. Thus by using his Maltese he could get into Arabic, and from Arabic he moved into Swahili. He had the ability to remember the different words immediately and to use them himself. This was a revelation to him, and he found mastering different languages an exciting challenge.

With their background of lush green coconut trees and surrounded by the bright blue sea, the many white sandy inlets, their fishing boats anchored out or pulled up onto the shore, made an inviting picture. The long narrow boats or *ingalawas* – dug out from tree trunks, and with a raised bow – had two outriggers.

Their single sail hoisted on a gaff rig that caught Martin's eye and roused his maritime curiosity. But the positive impressions of his first days of being in Zanzibar were soured by other realities. Walking up one of the narrow streets of Stone Town he saw a sight that sickened him to the core. A black boy, probably not more then ten years old, was carrying a heavy log on his head and the log was chained to his ankles. Martin was thus confronted face to face with slavery and found it difficult to understand. The sad, wide-open eyes of the boy were imprinted on his soul and he felt utter despair. The fact was that behind the closed ornate doors and barred windows of Zanzibar the majority of the black population were slaves. Indian traders owned about 8,000 and the Sultan 4,000 for his clove plantations; other Arab and black citizens owned between 500 and 2,000 slaves,[5] a situation that Livingstone, in his time, had spoken out so loud against.

The Europeans in Zanzibar numbered only a few dozen: the small staffs of the Consulates of Great Britain,

Germany and France, usually limited to one or two expatriates, and the few missionaries at the Church Missionary Society and Roman Catholic missions. When Martin arrived in Zanzibar Stone Town he contacted the British Consul, Sir John Kirk, and discussed the shipwreck with him. There was nothing that Kirk could do about it. The Sultan's administration – what there was of it – would not be in a position to take any action either. It was therefore up to the American skipper of the vessel to report the circumstances to the United States Consulate, but there is no record of any action having been taken as a result. Martin was billeted with the British sailors until arrangements could be made for his future. He disliked all forms of offensive action or fighting and would not join in the navy's task; anyway, he could not be absorbed into the Royal Navy, or receive any wages from that source. There was no regular calling of steamers at the island, and it could be a month or two before any arrived. He was anyway now sick and tired of going to sea, and the images he saw of any seafaring future were painted with a dark sky. The Church Missionary Society came to his rescue. There was no work for him in its Zanzibar mission, but the newly established ‘ centre in Mombasa, called Freretown, needed assistance. Like many before him, he cherished the relative comforts of Zanzibar, and it would became the civilised base from which he would venture into the mainland, but it was also quite easy for him to leave now in search of new experiences.

7 Learning in Africa 1880

Freretown, just north-west of Mombasa, was sorely in need of help to cope with the influx of Africans from various parts of East Africa who sought refuge there after escaping or being liberated from the Arab-led slave caravans. The town was named after Sir Bartle Frere, a former Governor of Bombay, who had helped push through the Anglo-Zanzibar treaty that abolished slave trading. Lieutenant Lloyd Mathews was just about to leave Zanzibar for Mombasa with a small company of local troops to establish new posts on the mainland. He offered Martin a passage, and on the journey the two got to know each other and struck up a friendship that was to last as long as both remained in East Africa.

Freretown was on the western or land end of Mombasa, and beyond it lay the African bush from which the tired and stricken slaves arrived. CMS not only gave refuge to those it welcomed but sought to rehabilitate them by teaching them the rudiments of a trade. Martin was given the task of general supervisor, and was able to make use of all he knew about sail-making, tailoring, carpentering and the other odd jobs that he had handled in the ships in which he had sailed in. He also learned how to excavate wells, build huts and set up a camp. The positioning of a camp away from flood danger and away from swamp wetland was the basis. The camp had, however, to be close to a water source such as a river, spring or well. He learned to allow for a slope and where to dig trenches to drain the camp in the heavy rains. The logistics of getting wooden poles and materials for the huts were part of the preparation. A hard wood (usually *mvuli*) was picked for the main columns of the hut, which were dug deep into the red soil to act as an anchor and stop the hut from being blown down in the high winds. Freshly cut wattle branches, stripped of their leaves, were then woven between the main posts. Strips of coconut palm leaf were used to tie everything together. The roof trusses, positioned to form an apex, were also of a hard wood and were tied, again with coconut palm leaf strips, to a kind of ring beam. Next the pitched roof was made by hanging coconut leaves (*makuti*) with the 'V' facing downwards to let the rain run off. Several layers were tied and built up. The wattle walls were infilled with wet mud – just soil mixed with water. This made the walls, once the sun had dried them out, as hard as stone. The final task was to create drains so that the water running off the roofs could be collected and made to run away from and not into the huts. The roofs had an overhang of two feet or more, providing shade for those sitting outside the hut.

The Kikuyu tribe, for example, had a strict rule that a hut had to be completed in a day, before sunset. It was believed that an unroofed hut could let in evil spirits at night and once they were in they couldn't be dislodged, so the roof was protection. Latrines were separate and were dug a distance from the huts. The whole camp, or *boma*, was protected from animals by an outer circular hedge of cut thorn bushes around the huts. Sometimes a large ditch was dug in front of the thorn bushes for protection and drainage purposes. There was a gap in the thorn bushes for the entrance, which was sealed by means of a gate. This was a building pattern Martin would repeat many times in the future and would become expert at. As some of the freed slaves were women and children, suitable separate accommodation had to be built for them. He soon found a certain satisfaction in helping and caring for the unfortunate inmates who had no home or family.

Martin had arrived in Zanzibar with little prior knowledge of the place and its history, and the short stay he had there allowed insufficient time for him to be inducted into the social mindset of the Europeans. He thus arrived at Freretown with an untainted, or perhaps naïve, view of Africans and in particular of slaves. He didn't have the common idea of white supremacy over black. His positive attitude would have been further enhanced by the CMS personnel themselves. His communication with the Africans could thus be without prejudice, and he was free of the prevailing view that slaves were 'wild savages'. Added to this, his Maltese background determined that he approached people with warmth and respect.

Although James Martin never learned to read or write, at Freretown he developed the knowledge of spoken Kiswahili and other African languages and dialects that was to prove invaluable to him in the various tasks and appointments he later held in East Africa. His natural talent and the few Swahili words he had learned in Zanzibar enabled him to communicate with his Swahili helpers. Martin realised that the different tribes that came to the town each spoke a different language and had different customs. As well as learning their languages, he took great interest in identifying the tribes from the looks and dress of the people. He respected the different greetings and manners of handshake, which were most important for the natives. Some handshakes were quite elaborate, and it became a sort of a game, rather like those he had played as a child. The handshake was only the beginning of the greeting, and although the languages were different the overall process was the same. The greeting words were the equivalent of *habari yako* ('how is your news?') in each of the languages. Commenting on the weather, or asking what town a person came from, was just not the done thing. The object of the greeting was to find out what tribe, or what family in the tribe, a person belonged to (that is, were they friend or foe). So the greeting would continue: 'How is the news of your family?' 'Fine' (*mazuri*) or just an *ahaa* was the reply. 'How is the news of your cousins?' to which the reply might again be *ahaa* – and so on, sometimes for minutes. Once one was sure that the other person was 'okay' the real news would start: 'However, we had a flood that devastated our village last month!' Greetings took time and delivered a lot of information if you knew how to read it.

This was the start of Martin's continuous quest for information about the native tribes. Although there were many tribes and sub-tribes, he eventually identified the five main ones. These were the Kikuyu, the Maasai, the Luhya, the Luo and the Swahili, and each had several sub- or associated tribes. The Kikuyu were of darker complexion and their language was Bantu-based. They were agriculturists and also animal herders. Martin found out that, traditionally, the women tended the crops and the men the cattle, sheep and goats. The extended family plot of land was an important possession and the basis of their livelihood. In his future travels through Kikuyuland he would be impressed by the work the women did and the loads they carried. Some of the older women had an indented band-mark across their foreheads where a hide strap had been tied. The strap would be attached to a bag that supported heavy loads such as fire wood or water. The women were, like many Kikuyu, hard-working and industrious. He remembered once thinking that a Kikuyu woman, bent forward carrying a heavy load of sticks up a hill, resembled an amazing ant bearing a stone several times its own size. The women wore pointed brown leather work aprons and just trudged on and on. This transport 'pack animal' existence took its toll on their bodies. Only the young women had straight figures and firm breasts; work gave the rest a bent demeanour with sagging breasts as they shuffled along. The Kikuyu had religious beliefs and a culture of government by a councils of elders. However, each section of the clan was relatively independent, so an agreement made with one chief did not necessarily hold with another. They tended often to have a group of elders as 'governors' rather than a single chief.

Just as Africa had different languages, it also had different smells, difficult to describe: dry, peppery, perhaps coffee-like, heavy and deep, together with the native body odour of fat and red ochre that was rubbed on, giving a sort of rancid aroma. Tribes that were heavier meat eaters, like those from Lake Victoria Nyanza, had a stronger, muskier and perhaps less pleasant odour (and it was said that you could tell a cannibal by his smell). Other more vegetarian tribes, like the Kikuyu, were less pungent. Smells became identified with places and people and were a language in themselves which activated the mind with images, memory and sometimes instant emotions.

The Maasai had a generally redder complexion and straighter facial features. They were mainly semi-nomadic and herded their cattle from one pasture area to another. Some of them, like the Chagga, were more agriculturist than nomad. Their cattle were sacred to them and were seldom killed as they were a symbol of wealth. Cattle also provided the Maasai with vital vitamins. Martin had sometimes been offered blood from a cow's neck to drink. A slit was made in a vein in the neck and the blood collected in a vessel. The slit was sealed by being pressed tightly once enough blood had been taken. In this way the Maasai could continually drink fresh blood. In many respects their whole lives revolved around the needs of their cattle. In the rainy season, when the plains were lush and green, the cattle would be put out to graze. Towards the end of the rains the tribe would move with their cattle towards the rivers that provided water for the dryer time of the year. This cycle of annual migration was shared with the millions of wildlife, like the wildebeest, zebras and the lions that followed them. The Maasai needed a vast area of land so that their cattle could move around. If a path were blocked by a farm it would mean trouble. Hence the Maasai concept of land ownership was different from that of the other agriculturist tribes. This meant that there was potential for conflict with land-fixed tribes such as the Kikuyu or Luo.

A Maasai group, or *kraal*, was a polygamous family compound. About twenty of these *kraals* made up a village or *boma*. The males were divided into three groups according to age: youths, warriors (*moran*), and elders. When youths became warriors, they moved to a different type of village, called a *manyatta*. In the *manyatta* lived the warriors, their mothers and sisters and uninitiated girls. In contrast, the *kraal* was made up of families of married elders. The older male warriors went through a long process (up to six months) of handing over the warrior status to the younger incomers, before they got married and joined the elders. There was great peer pressure on the younger ones to prove that they were suitable warriors, and it was during this time that most fighting broke out with neighbouring tribes. The young men had relative autonomy within the tribe and in these times the elders had little influence on them. Understanding these dynamics – that they were mostly 'young lads' on the rampage – helped Martin in interacting with and influencing them. The Maasai warriors had a reputation for being fierce fighters, but Martin got to know them as straightforward, humorous people.

Luhya tribal life, on the other hand, revolved around the extended family where polygamy was the norm, and this was fascinating to any European. There was a strict hierarchy among the men of the tribe; women had little status and could not own land, but were seen as eventual 'possessions' of their future husbands. When a Luhya inhabitant of the town died, all his fellow tribesmen came and celebrated around his hut for what seemed like days. They went into the nearby forest and uprooted a large tree, and buried him under the spot. They then went on to plant a new, smaller tree next to the uprooted one.

The Luo were another tribe Martin managed to get to know at this time and about which he would learn more in the future. He found them a versatile and industrious folk who were quick to smile and often liked to play music and dance. One day a young Luo arrived at the Freretown camp looking rather poorly. He had been snatched from his village near Lake Victoria, in the dead of night, by a group of native raiders. Although he was a brave fighter, when the 'night spirits', who wore strange masks, woke him up and pointed spears in his face, he had frozen in fear and been unable do anything. It was as if his whole will to act had drained out of him. He could not understand why he had behaved so passively – it was as if he were programmed to do so. He was tied up by the raiders and marched for two weeks to an area further inland, where he was sold to Arab traders in exchange for a few cattle. The traders put him in chains and he walked the two-and-a-half-month journey to the coast carrying a load of ivory tusks. His friend who had been chained next to him died halfway through the march. The slave trader had just unhooked his chains in the morning and dragged the body away.

On arrival at the coast, he and the other slaves that were still alive were put in a dark cave where they waited for a week. The young Luo had never felt so sad, but there was nothing he could do. He was herded onto a dhow early one morning and chained to the galley below the deck. Two days into the sailing, he heard shouting as another ship came alongside. Sailors in blue coats boarded the dhow and came down to the galley, where they cut the slaves' chains and set them free. Within two days he had arrived in Freretown. Martin asked the young man what his name was.

'Barak,' he replied, in a half-frightened voice. Martin tried as usual to link the new word with a similar-sounding

Maltese one. He often found that he hit on a matching meaning, more as a joke then anything else.

'*Ahlla Ei Berak,*' he said, which was a common Maltese greeting-word that his mother always used, meaning 'God bless you'. Barak's eyes lit up and a smile came to his face – his first smile in a long time.

Martin got along well with the young man for the rest of his time in Freretown. He learned a little of the Luo language, and something of the people's culture and their ways of fishing and working. The other man learned the skills Martin taught him and slowly regained his self-respect.

As Martin got to know more about the various tribes, he found that there were many similarities between them. However, they differed in details that were important to those involved. The people lived in family groups, several of which made up the tribe. The family was seen in a wide context to include not just husband and wife (or husband and wives in some of the tribes like the Lou and Luhya), children and parents, but also cousins and 'blood brothers'. The family bond was important. Most tribes had a council of elders who chose a chief often after several rounds of voting. Once picked, the chief carried much authority and was always the best 'contact' in a tribe. Consultations among the elders over the decreeing of laws were a check on the chief's authority. The chief could in most tribes be deposed by the elders' council if he broke certain rules regarding drunkenness, quarrelling and overeating or attempted to govern without regard to the input of the elders. So there was a form of democracy. These tribes had a long history. The more Martin learned about it, the more interested he became and the more respect he had for the indigenous people. The tribes had migrated from different areas to 'discover' suitable regions in which to live, sometimes fighting to take them over. They had hierarchies among themselves, with one tribe looking down on another – usually the stronger looking down on the weaker. These things suggested why fighting began between tribes, but they didn't really explain why conflict persisted continually.

Taboos and superstitions were

part of the culture. The 'medicine man' or 'witch doctor' was the figure that instilled the fear of 'night runners' or 'spirit men' who came and took people away. There was indeed always a real fear that, from one day to the next, they might be pulled into slavery. And slavery was the very worst thing. Martin's first perceptions of Zanzibar, with its illegal but still active slave trade, were imprinted in his memory. He learned about the evil politics of the trade carried on with the upcountry tribes, and understood that it poisoned their lives and their culture and was the major cause for mistrust between tribes.

The East African tribes had, for over 300 years, suffered from the slave trade. Trafficking had grown from 10,000 slaves a year in 1811 to about 40,000 in 1839, with an estimated peak of 70,000 slaves being sold in 1860. Although trading slaves was made illegal in 1873 by the Anglo-Zanzibar treaty, illegal trading continued into the 1880s. Slavery itself remained legal until 1897 in Pemba, until 1907 in the coast region and as late as 1921 – the start of the British mandate – in

Tanganyika. The main slave traders in James Martin's time were the coast Arabs and the Swahili coast people; years before them it had been the Portuguese, Dutch and British, who operated mainly from the west coast of Africa. The Arabs and Swahili had over the years made Zanzibar their 'safe base' from which they carried out their slave trading, initially on the coast. Eventually, they had to venture into the very heart of Africa to plunder their slaves. The users of slaves, or the 'market', were the plantations (cloves, cotton, fruit, palm oil, grain and gum copra) in Zanzibar and elsewhere around the world, which depended on this labour to run their new industries. The Mombasa area employed almost 50,000 slaves in plantations at that time. Domestic slavery in Arabia and elsewhere was another market, as was sexual slavery, and slaves were used to transport ivory and ebony, wild animal skins and palm oil from inside Africa to the coast. The slave trade affected almost every tribe and depopulated large areas. Quite often African tribes such as the Nyamwezi, who lived between Lake Victoria and Lake Rukwa, would capture people from their fellow tribes and make them slaves, trading with the Arab and Swahili traders or even with other tribal chiefs. Livingstone had highlighted this problem in around 1866:

Livingstone asked the locals repeatedly why they found it necessary to sell their people to a handful of intruders, and was told: 'If so and so gives up selling so will we.' 'He is the greatest offender in the country, it is the fault of the Arabs who tempt us with fine clothes, powder, and guns.' 'I will fain keep all my people to cultivate more land, but my neighbour allows his people to kidnap mine and I must have ammunition to defend them.'[6]

The Kore tribe was defeated by the Maasai in a fight and all the survivors were plundered by a Somali tribe and taken as slaves. They were eventually freed by the British who settled them on the island of Lamu.

The fear of slavery affected the whole psyche of the Africans and bred helplessness, apathy, hatred and inter-tribal wars, with the stronger tribes trying to kill and plunder the weaker. Kings or chiefs traded their subjects, conquerors traded their captives, courts traded those they had sentenced. This led to an inferiority complex that in turn made slavery easier. [7] Prices recorded were $1 for a child, $12 for a beautiful young girl; at this time one horse sold for twelve slaves. Later on prices of $70 to $100 for a female were recorded. Ivory was the other main trading commodity. The trade in itself was passable as long as there was a surplus of animals and the local people benefited from the meat. (Today's conservationists would disagree, but in those times too many elephants could be a menace.) However, slaves were often used to transport the ivory, and hence it was part of the vicious circle that developed in many tribes, with cattle being stolen to pay for ivory that would be carried by slaves, either traded or captured. Cattle were the internal currency for paying the natives, ivory and slaves the export goods taken by the foreigners.[8]

Although the trading of slaves had recently been made illegal (the United States had abolished slavery from their constitution fifteen years earlier, in 1865), it was still legal to hold slaves. This made it very difficult for traders to be captured, unless they were caught red-handed. They only had to plead ownership for things to be legal. Trading was thus driven underground, which made conditions for the slaves even worse. Transport in the interior was slow and by foot, so that once a caravan of slaves was taken they disappeared into the unknown and were difficult to find. The task of redeeming the scourge of slavery seemed almost impossible at the time.

These are all things Martin learned at Freretown, and was to understand more of in the years to come. His time in Freretown gave him a unique introduction to the tribes, areas and languages of Africa. He was probably better versed in the different native languages then any European before him, even though he was illiterate. Learning made him less apprehensive of meeting the indigenous people and of what lay ahead in 'darkest Africa'. He admired the simplicity and humour of the people, with which he could connect. He was able to make them laugh and he responded to their humour. It was the start of his quest for knowledge, and the assistance he gave them would continue. Freretown was no university but was the closest the dyslexic, illiterate Martin would get to a training environment. His dyslexic mind remembered everything in all its detail, and some of the rough edges he possessed were smoothed over.

8 Exploring the Maasailand (1883–1884)

Every month or two Martin made the journey by dhow to visit the CMS mission back in Zanzibar, built on the site previously occupied by the slave market. He also liked to renew acquaintance with Lieutenant Lloyd Mathews and with the crew of HMS *London*, whose captain had recently been murdered by slavers off the island of Pemba. He had been succeeded by Captain Brownrigg, and Martin now wished to meet the new senior naval officer in order to keep open a possible line of travel back to Europe. It was on one of his visits to Zanzibar that Martin met Joseph Thomson, the geologist and explorer. Thomson had arrived there from England on 26 January 1883, with the declared aim of opening up the direct route from Mombasa to Uganda. Africa was, of course, not completely unknown in Thomson's time, but the geography of Central Africa had always been a mystery to Europeans, as it had been to the Greeks and Romans, and prior to Livingstone there was no knowledge of the Great Lakes or the source of the Nile river. David Livingstone, the first great explorer, crossed Africa along the line of the Zambesi (latitude approximately 10° South) in 1853 and 1856. Two years later, in 1858, Richard Burton and John Speke reached Lake Tanganyika (approximately 5° South). Speke also in that year went north and sighted the Great Lake that he called Victoria Nyanza. He returned to the area in 1862 with James Grant and went up the western side of the lake to discover the Ripon Falls (just 0.5° North). In 1864 Samuel Baker reached Luta Nzige, a lake north-west of Speke's

Victoria Nyanza, or Lake Victoria, and called it Lake Albert.

All the Great Lakes had thus been discovered to Europeans, but the extent to which they were linked up was not clear. It seemed conceivable that Lake Tanganyika could be the Nile's source. It was left to Henry Morton Stanley, in 1874–77, to link all these lakes and define Lake Victoria as the source of the Nile. However, Stanley passed by the western shores of the Kavirondo region without visiting it, hence at this time the whole area to the east of Lake Victoria, from latitude 5° South, up to just above the equator, was still unknown. This was Thomson's target area. German explorers had been very active to the south and east of Mount Kilimanjaro, signing treaties with local African chiefs by which their territories were placed under the protection of the German flag, and Thomson wanted to forestall them to the north. The unexplored area that was the target of Thomson's expedition lay between Mount Kilimanjaro and Lake Victoria and included territory peopled by the wild and bellicose Maasai, feared by all who ventured near them. Their country had in fact been scrupulously avoided by Arab slavers and traders. A few years earlier, an entire caravan led by an Arab named Mbaruk had been massacred by Maasai. Close to the Maasai lived the unpredictable and equally dangerous Kikuyu tribe.

Motivated in part by Edinburgh University, which wanted to compete with its rival Glasgow University, where Livingstone had studied, Thomson had planned his expedition some years before. He had been in Zanzibar in 1881, and had then returned to England to seek backing for his venture (which he got from the Royal Geographical Society) and to buy the necessary stores and equipment. He had decided to travel inland in East Africa without any white companions, but as he started to organise his caravan in Zanzibar he came across numerous problems. At this juncture he met James Martin and was impressed by his knowledge of the coastal people and his command of their languages. Martin had very good certificates of character reliability from the British Consul and the CMS mission, and no doubt Lloyd Mathews and the officers of HMS *London* also helped. So Thomson engaged Martin as his second-in-command and put him to work to find the porters for their caravan.

Martin seems to have had no binding ties with the CMS mission at Freretown to prevent him from changing his job, and he threw himself into this new appointment with enthusiasm. He was keen to experience the mainland he had heard so much about from those who came to Frere Town. The expedition was to turn out a great success and, thanks to Thomson's lavish praise of him, to build his reputation as an incomparable safari caravan organiser and leader. At the end of January 1883, Thomson went over to the mainland at Pangani with Martin to reconnoitre the initial stages of their forthcoming safari. They walked for six hours along the coast to Mombasa, and Thomson was disappointed to see that Martin was not a good walker and had skinned his heels badly. This did not augur well for the future, but on this occasion it was put down to badly fitting shoes. The numerous stores for the journey were brought to a depot at Tanga, which had a good harbour for dhows, and Martin came into his own steering the dhows along the coastal waters and in and out of the tricky coral reefs. It was not until 3 March 1883 that the caravan actually set off from Zanzibar, assembled on the mainland opposite Rabai (nearer Mombasa) and, with all the fuss and cacophony of such a large and excited gathering of askaris and hangers-on, commenced its exploration safari marching behind the Union Jack and the red flag of the Sultan of Zanzibar. They were taking the more common southerly 'German route' into the interior.

There were over a hundred men in Thomson's Victoria Nyanza and Mount Kenya Expedition, and three donkeys to carry the sick or injured if the occasion arose. The porters carried loads weighing the regulation 65 to 70 pounds; these were balanced on their heads, and it was uncanny to observe how the men moved, swerved, climbed and even ran without unbalancing their loads. Nearly half of the baggage contained items to be used as gifts for the natives – thirty-four loads of iron, brass or copper wire, fourteen loads of bales of cloth, and as many as twenty-nine containers of beads. Then there were the tents, tent furniture, clothing, boots and personal stores, including scientific equipment and five cases of ammunition. (Although some dry provisions were also carried, the main supply of food was expected to come from wild animals shot en route.) As the contents were used up, the loads would be lightened uniformly. The porters received three months' pay on departure, and there was a strong temptation, in the initial stages of the safari, for them to defect from the lines, with or without their load, especially at night-time. To prevent this, the caravan included a dozen armed soldiers – the askaris – who also provided the column's security against wild animals and aggressive natives.

Thomson was in no hurry. He first wanted to visit the chiefs of the populated areas at the foot of Mount Kilimanjaro. These lay in the path of the caravans – missionaries, explorers, traders and slavers who had previously travelled inland to Central Africa and round the back of Lake Victoria to Ruanda and Uganda – and were well known. Thomson thus decided it would be worth his while to cultivate their friendship and obtain as much information as he could about the Maasai, the Kikuyu and their territory. Furthermore, a British presence in the disputed area south of the mountain in that delicate period could not but dampen the competitive tendencies of the German explorers. The caravan moved slowly to Taveta and stayed there for some time. In May the first move was made to enter the uncharted country of the Maasai, but they were soon warned that their path ahead was blocked by 2,000 warriors on the warpath. Thomson retreated rapidly to Taveta. After consulting Martin, he decided to travel back to Mombasa to fetch more porters and askaris and additional stores, while Martin looked after the bulk of the caravan and the equipment during his absence. Left to his own devices, Martin lost no time in communicating with the surrounding chiefs and exerting his charm. He became a blood brother of some of them and won favours from others. He made friendships that would prove helpful on future safaris. He bought a sizeable plot of land at Taveta by the side of a stream, and built a *baraza*, or assembly hall, in the centre with a flagpole flying the British flag. Near by, he constructed a dwelling for himself and a series of huts for his *askaris* and safari leaders and porters. When Thomson returned to Taveta he declared himself astonished and full of admiration as he was led into the center of a pretty, rustic village where before had stood the rankest jungle. He could hardly believe that these were his quarters and that the whole transformation was Martin's work:

"I was soon conducted inside our cosy grass-built house, and while refreshing the outer and inner man, I listened with intense interest to Martin's tale of trial and trouble.'[9]

Martin had in fact had some difficulty with Chief Mandara, the head of the Wa-Chagga clan, who had the reputation of being savage and bloodthirsty. While they were confined to camp at Taveta during Thomson's absence in Mombasa, food reserves had run alarmingly low. Mandara, learning this, invited Martin to visit him, but Martin was wary. He first sent one of his headmen, who happily returned with some food; then he summoned courage to go himself. He found Mandara to be most approachable and friendly, and the life of the little camp became much easier. It was through Mandara that Martin obtained a plot of land on which to construct the stockade that so impressed Thomson on his return from Mombasa. So it was natural for Thomson to invite Chief Mandara to visit the expedition's camp and to present him with gifts.

The month of fasting – Ramadhan – had now ended. (The majority of the coast Arabs were Muslim, and so were some of the coast porters.) It was already August, and it was time to face up to the journey into Maasailand. Hundreds of coloured beads had been strung into the customary length for the Maasai (any other lengths would have been rejected), and cloth had been cut and sewn in the manner they found acceptable. This time there were no alarms, and it seemed that the previous risk of a confrontation with Maasai Moran had been invented with the aim of bringing the expedition back to Taveta. While the

Maasai women scurried out of their way, the older men were pleased to meet Thomson and Martin and raised no objection to their proceeding with the journey towards Victoria Nyanza, provided that they did not harm the cattle, caused no trouble and travelled in peace. Gifts of beads, wire and cloth had to be distributed as *chango* – a kind of transit fee – gauged according to the importance of the Maasai chief encountered. The Europeans in the caravan were the subject of much curiosity, and frequently had to suffer embarrassing personal inspection by the Moran – the arrogant and contemptuous teenagers of the Maasai, who roamed the countryside in aggressive spear-waving groups, fearless of any opponent, until they had blooded their spears. The clothes and boots of the intruders were handled with guffaws and frivolity, hats knocked awry, and efforts made to snatch any loose object or unattended load.

So the expedition proceeded, rising early to be on the march, with Thomson leading and Martin bringing up the rear; a halt after two hours for a brief rest; a meeting with Maasai tending their large herds of cattle or a chat with little groups who gathered around the strangers. (The inevitable Maasai greeting of spitting at the ground – on introduction, on agreeing to something and on departure – is an expression of goodwill, and some filed a gap between their two front teeth to facilitate this.) Then on with the journey – at times tough and slow, at times covering twenty miles a day, and on one special occasion no less than seventy miles in one day. Obstacles that arose in their path could be formidable: rivers to be bridged; mountains to be climbed or circumvented; dense forests to be cut through; ravines to be traversed; steep escarpments to be negotiated; interminable thorn bushes to be avoided; days of waterless and shadeless desert to be crossed; and, not least, the constant threat from unpredictable wild game.

Martin never ceased to be amazed at the beauty of the vast open spaces. With the daily hard trek and enthusiastic organisation that occupied his whole being, he particularly savoured the relaxation of dusk and dawn. The rising of the sun, which happens so quickly in the tropics, was the best part of the day. The sun comes in horizontally and lights up the vertical lines of trees, animals and people. They are clearer and crisper, and the light brings out all the subtle tones that are lost when the hot sun is overhead and melts the trees into the surrounding ground, blanking or blending out the natural colours as on overexposed film; the vertical lines are lost in the onslaught of heat and light of the African sun. Faces appear mellower while the dawn lasts.

There was an abundance of game in the plains of Maasailand. Besides zebra, wildebeest and impala, there were hundreds of smaller gazelle. One of the more beautiful and graceful of these caught Thomson's eye. It was small, about 80 centimetres tall – roughly half the size of a zebra – and had a light brown coat with a white underside and a distinctive black stripe. The animal's horns were long, ribbed and pointed, with an elegant gentle curve. The white patch on the rump extended to underneath the tail. A noticeable behaviour was the gazelle's bounding leap, which it used to startle predators. The creatures ate the low vegetation and grass of the savannah grasslands and their water intake came mostly from the grass they ate. They would be named after Thomson himself: *Gazella thomsoni*, or Thomson's gazelle. Animals were shot to provide food for the caravan, but it always seemed a shame when one of these creatures was killed. They could be semi-tame, and were often seen eating grass close to the huts that Martin would later establish.

Thomson had decided to go on a diversion to Mount Kenya and left Martin in charge of the safari for a couple of weeks. After inspecting Mount Kenya, Thomson discovered the falls that are named after him. He then rejoined the caravan, going on to discover Lake Baringo. His expedition continued to Kavirondo and reached the town of Mumias (or Kwa Sundu). It then proceeded a short distance south-west to reach the eastern shores of Lake Victoria (Victoria Nyanza). (This part of the journey would have passed just north of the present-named town of Ndori, the home land of Barack Obama's ancestors.) The scene when they reached the lake was described by Thomson in his book *Through Masai Land*:

An hour's feverish tramp, almost breaking into a run, served to bring us to the edge of Lake Victoria Nyanza, and soon we were joyously drinking deep draughts of its waters, while the men ran in knee-deep, firing their guns and splashing about like madmen.

The main objective of the expedition set for him by the Royal Geographical Society had now been achieved: he had discovered the last remaining important secrets of Central Africa. Knowing this, Thomson, full of pride, gave a speech to his group 'on heroic lines more commonly heard at a city banquet or Mutual Admiration Society than in central Africa'. Their duty carried out, they then turned back and proceeded to the nearby village of the second chief of Samia (part of the Lou tribe), and part of Kavirondo. They entered the village still in high spirits.

The last piece of the puzzle of the geographical aspects of Africa had now been discovered, and relevant links on maps substantiated by the western world. It seemed like the last chapter in a book, with this village visit being the final full stop. It was, however, only the prelude to a far more significant historical journey, not linking up geography but linking up people.

9 From Lake Victoria to the White House in three generations

Martin and Thomson had no idea what they were setting in motion by their visit to this Luo tribe towards the end of 1883. They were, as far as we know, the very first white men the tribe had ever seen, and precisely one year later, in 1884, Hussein Onyango Obama was born to the Luo. His would be the first generation to take advantage of the opportunities these white men brought with them, and it was as a direct result of the educational possibilities thereby created that Onyango's grandson, just over a century later, would be sworn in as the forty-fourth president of the United States of America on 20 January

2009. Only two generations of the family separated the first steps of white men among the Luo and a descendant of the Luo becoming leader of the most powerful country in the world.

The Luo are an old tribe, well established since leaving their original territories in Wau, Sudan, 350 years ago, and following the rivers and lakes that provided the fish they depended upon as their staple food. They were at first neither truly nomadic nor truly settled, moving on when the fishing became poor, or the land became overpopulated, or when they were driven out by neighbouring warring tribes. Whatever the reasons, they eventually reached Lake Victoria, the source of the great River Nile, and here, under the influence of their powerful chieftain Ramogi Ajwang, they stayed, laying claim to 1,000 kilometres of shoreline, around the year 1500.

And then it was that the Luo began to flourish and lay down the traditions that Onyango Obama would be born into, and that James Martin and Joseph Thomson would observe at close quarters when they arrived. Had either been anthropologists, instead of the former being an illiterate Swahili-speaking sailor and the latter an educated Glaswegian geologist with itchy feet, they might have noted that the Luo tribe's traditions fell into roughly four areas or zones: Ancestor, Social, Work and Spirit.

The Ancestor zone provided the general framework for the tribe: their history and collective oral knowledge passed down through families. A person would never describe himself or herself merely by their given name, but also as 'the son of …' or 'the daughter of …', thus placing themselves truly in tribal family tree.

The Social zone provided them with the structures that keep a community together: shared ceremonies, initiation rites, marriage rituals and so on. Each tribal chief lived in a *boma* – a collection of several huts – with his extended clan and relations. There would be separate huts for each of his wives and her family, all crowded together, sleeping on woven raffia mats on the floor. The richer a man was, the more wives he had, and the more livestock. One interesting tradition among the wives was a collective uprising against the power of their men, when every two months they would band together and go off in a noisy convoy to shout and scream at neighbouring tribes. No violence ensued, apart from a severe tongue-lashing, as if they had saved up their daily frustrations and then vented them all at once.

There were also the dancing parties, *ngomas*, when the women, naked from the waist up, would perform their routines, jumping, singing, clapping and ululating, sensual or trance-like depending on the occasion. James Martin and Joseph Thomson viewed this close up, and indeed joined in on one occasion, as Thomson writes in *Through Masai Land*:

> Finding ourselves among very pleasant people, we laid aside our natural reserve and, pocketing our high dignity … illustrated the Poetry of Motion as practiced in Malta and Scotland; that is to say, Martin tried to initiate the damsels into the mysterious charm of the waltz [the Maltija Dance] while I showed them how to do the 'fantastic' in the spirited movement of the Scotch dance. Need I say that Martin was simply nowhere, while

> they became enthusiastic over my performance. That night, as I sat musing and star-gazing, I concluded that the Wa-Kavirondo [the Luo] were decidedly susceptible of civilising influences.[10]

It is an extraordinary scene to imagine, these two white men, the first the Luo had ever seen, trying to teach the bare-breasted women how to waltz and dance the light fantastic, and it says much about why the Martin/Thomson duo were so successful. They were willing to integrate themselves and to learn, and never once, so Thomson claimed, did they have to fire a shot in anger throughout the whole of their 3,000-mile expedition. These were men who went to the bother of learning the Nilotic dialect spoken by the Luo, and who thought nothing of flinging caution to the wind and joining in whenever they were asked. It is also obvious from Thomson's comments that he not only accepted the Luo's way of life, but positively admired it. This is especially evident in terms of the third zone, which comprises the world of Work.

Much of the daily labour about the camp, was carried out by the women, particularly during the course of food preparation. The Luo were at this time still principally dependent on fish for their protein, but had also developed an agriculture based largely around the cropping of the abundant banana plants. Every morning the women would go down to the shore and catch silver perch in woven baskets. (These fish are flattish in appearance, and up to two feet in length.) They were gutted and then staked onto sticks that had been carefully stuck into the ground about their fires so that the soft flesh was closest to the flames. Once cooked, the fish were filled with herbs and vegetables, closed up and thrown onto the edges of the fires so that the skin would burn and hold the package together. These were served with green bananas that had been sliced, boiled and mashed, along with some herbs, or occasionally with some cultivated corn ground into flour and made into flat breads.

So much, so usual: a realm of work and food that was common to almost every tribe living up and down the shores of Lake Victoria. But what intrigued Joseph Thomson most about the Luo tribe was what set them apart from their peers, for they had developed an industrial expertise that was unique in the whole of Central Africa: they had become metal workers, and very skilled ones at that. As Thomson enthusiastically puts it:

We found numerous smelting works, the ore being brought from regular mines, in a range of hills to the north. They smelted it in open furnaces of charcoal, heaped up against a low wall, at the bottom of which is a hole and a drain leading from it to carry slag. The blast is kept up by a double bellows, worked with astonishing dexterity, by a man standing. A whole day is employed in smelting the ore, and a mass of 15–20 lbs is the result. The moment it is thought to be ready they turn out the hot mass and as speedily as possible cut pieces off with axes, dealing with great rapidity [and] Herculean strokes. The iron thus produced is first class, and the [Loa], especially those of Samia, are remarkably clever blacksmiths. They make rings of beautifully polished metal worn by the young around their necks and legs … [and] spears, arrow heads, hammers, hoes and other weapons and utensils, which were used all around their country.

It is no wonder that Thomson was so impressed; the Luo's mastery of smelting iron ore must have seemed near miraculous to their neighbouring tribes who did not possess the knowledge, and would have given them a trading edge that others lacked. It may also have given the elders of the Luo tribes a bit of a bargaining chip against another, most formidable, bearer of power within the tribal structure, namely the witchdoctor. It was he who presided over the fourth and final zone, which comprised the Spiritual well-being of the Luo.

The role of the witchdoctor is familiar to the modern-day reader: a man who had knowledge of plants and rudimentary medicines, but a man also more akin to a magician than a true medicine man because much of his power was in his ability to perform. Done in the right way, for example, the *dawa ya ku lala* (Swahili for 'sleeping medicine') rite could be enough to put a man to sleep in a moment by the mere power of suggestion; in the wrong hands, it was just a man tying a couple of little bones together and chanting a few incoherent words. We are sceptical today of such men and their tricks, though in many places in the world they still hold sway over their populace. It was by the appearance of men like James Martin and Joseph Thomson into their midst – along with their more modern and potent medicines – that their thrall first began to be slowly being broken. Of course, they often acted for the good of their tribes, and there is no doubt that many believed in their own powerful magic. If they played their role well, it was an easy thing to convince people that a specific man or woman was cursed, sometimes to such a degree that the cursed individual believed it too, and withered away and died. They could also exploit the fact that everyone in the region – Bantu, Maasai and Luo alike – were subject to the constant fear of being abducted and sold into slavery. The witchdoctor could go into a ranting trance, and call down night-raiders onto the village for some perceived sin or other, secure in the knowledge that at some time in the not too distant future such a raid would be sure to occur. More disturbingly, there is a good deal of evidence that many chiefs and their witchdoctors directly participated in the slave trade by selling off members of their own tribe, or those they had captured from their neighbours, for the purpose of consolidating their own power and wealth.

Inter-tribal theft, both of livestock and of people, was not an uncommon occurrence, and casts an interesting light on an incident that happened to Martin and Thomson during their visit to the Luo. Things appeared to have been going well, so they were much surprised to find that some of their possessions had been stolen from their tent while they were away. It was one of several times during their visits to the Maasai and Luo tribes that this petty thievery occurred, and it says much for our explorers that they didn't immediately react with force on any of these occasions, but instead chose to talk to the tribal elders about the problem, usually with the positive result of their not only getting back their goods but also gaining the tribe's respect for displaying tact, prudence and good character. As Thomson himself says of one such incident:

This adventure curiously enough seemed distinctly to raise us in the good-will of the people … [and by] the afternoon we were such excellent friends that they stood without fear to be photographed …

We can see from all this that James Martin and Joseph Thomson, the first white men ever to be seen by the Luo tribe, were received well, and departed better.

In the course of their entire expedition through the region, they experienced no major antagonistic events. It seems that their knowledge of the language – Martin's in particular – and their tolerant, open-handed attitudes earned them respect and liking. In fact the most dramatic part of the whole trek came when they were journeying back to Mombasa from their first visit to Lake Victoria. By this time they had been away for over a year; they had beaten the odds, and were among the few European travellers in this region who hadn't died either from disease or by attack. Malaria was a constant threat – in a previous expedition to the Niger in 1833, thirty-eight out of the forty-seven Britons (80%) died from it, and again when Henry Morton Stanley set off to search for Livingstone, many of his white companions succumbed. It is entirely possible that the

Maltese-born James Martin had more than luck on his side in this respect for there is a genetic aspect to malarial resistance known as the beta thalassaemia trait, which is particularly prevalent in Mediterranean people of Italian descent – as are many Maltese.

Be that as it may, James and Joseph's expedition was an unqualified success on all counts – until, that is, Thomson put himself in the path of an angry buffalo and got badly gored. His understanding of the behaviour of wild animals, buffalos in particular, was unfortunately not as good as his grasp of human dynamics. Having wounded the buffalo, he was tracking it down so as not to leave it in pain. Now, it is a common tactic among African buffalos, particularly when being pursued by a perceived enemy in bushy savannah country, to double back on their pursuers rather than follow the usual animal instinct to run away from the danger. Waiting in ambush for Thomson, the buffalo charged him from the side, catching him unawares and with no time to aim his weapon. This tactic makes buffalos still one of the most dangerous animals to hunt in Africa. It was a grievous blow, and Thomson was ill for many, many weeks. Having survived the initial wounding he went on to develop dysentery. They had no medicines left, and the men were anxious not to tarry in the bush now that they were on their way home. There is no doubt that, had it not been for James Martin's constant care and the controlling hand of discipline he had over his men, Thomson would have died. But he did not die, and eighteen months after they had set out from Mombasa they returned triumphant.

Throughout his memoirs of the expedition Joseph Thomson speaks highly of James Martin, to whom he owed much of the success of the expedition, not to mention his life.

I never had any reason to regret my decision to take him. Though unable to read or write he was very intelligent and could talk about ten languages in sailor fashion. In every respect [of] manners, language, dressing etc. he was far above the average sailor, and from the first I never scrupled to treat him as a companion … we never once had an unpleasantness between us [and] if it were ever my lot to go back to Africa, I would seek for no better assistant …

Although Joseph Thomson did not return to Africa, James Martin certainly did. This first expedition had opened up the boat route to Uganda and James Martin regularly used the route to reach Entebbe over the next ten years – one of the increasing volume of visitors to bring in new trade and innovative ideas.

In 1894 Martin returned to the area with a man named C. W. Hobley, and the following year this same C. W. Hobley was put in charge of the newly established trading station established by the British at Mumias. He would later be integral to the British efforts to stop inter-tribal fighting in the area, leading an expedition of a very different nature to the one undertaken by Martin and Thomson and tasked with keeping the peace in the areas of Sakwa, Seme and Uyoma. By this time the British were well established, and James Martin well established with them. He became a Government Administrator, and a name very well connected and very well known.

But this chapter of the Luo/Martin story is not quite at an end, for following the establishment of the station at

Mumias, the railway was pushed on into the interior of Uganda and had reached Port Florence in Kisumu by 1901. Two years later Port Florence was the terminus for a whole network of railways reaching across the land. Missionaries soon moved in, and with the missionaries came schools. In 1915 the Luo Chief Odera Akang'o was so impressed by what he saw of the British settlement and schooling system at Kampala that he decided to establish a similar system at his home in Gem – exactly the kind of school that Barack Obama's father attended less than a decade later. It might be said that none of this would have happened if it hadn't been for James Martin and Joseph Thomson's expedition to the shores of Lake Victoria in 1883. Not bad for an illiterate sailor from Malta: perhaps not quite as illustrious as the rise of the Obamas from Luo tribesmen to occupants of the White House, but surely just as astonishing and as worthy of praise.

10 Why Obama?

Yes, why was it a man from Western Kenya, the heart of Africa, that became the first black president and not, as would have been expected, a follower of Malcolm X, or a descendent of Martin Luther King, or a Jesse Jackson man or woman?

When Barak Obama started campaigning for the presidential election, there were even some quarters of the black population who said that he "wasn't Black". He hadn't been through the black civil rights movement, that black Americans had to fight through, so he couldn't really represent the blacks, he was an outsider. Of course, he was, eventually endorsed by black leaders as being "Black". This however highlighted an important point which made it clear that Barak Obama was somehow a different person, which made him an electable President. What were these differences and how did they come about?

In order to understand we need to go back to the roots, not only Obama's roots but also those of "black Americans".

So what was happening back in 1883, was a sort of start gun for the race to be the first black President.

The Blacks in the USA in the late 1800 were having a difficult time, Abraham Lincoln had lived and died, and the end of the Civil war (1865) had come. However these major events didn't seem to have much positive impact on the wellbeing of the blacks. In 1883, the United States Supreme Court, even ruled that the Civil Rights act of 1875, which forbid discrimination, in hotels and public places, was unconstitutional. The Civil Rights gained had thus been overturned. There was constant lynching of black men with out due legal process. It was an environment in which victimhood was a reality and hence not far off from the degradation of slavery. This was the social and mental environment that the Blacks had to move from, it would be a continual and hard struggle, against poverty and prejudice, leaving mental scars that would not be easy to get rid of.

The Blacks, on the other hand, in the Luo tribe in Western Kenya, on the Eastern shores of Lake Victoria, in 1883, were in their own element, ruled their own territory, and were one of the more advanced and prosperous tribes. They had had their own history of hardship in bringing their tribe to where they were at that time., but they had succeeded in establishing their sustainability, on their own. No external Western influence had reached them. So one can imagine culturally and mentally they were in a strong place, with a positive sense of wellbeing and contentment. (of course not everything was perfect). It was nevertheless, a far cry from the mental being of their United States counterparts.

The difference can perhaps best be explained, psychologically as the "locus of control". "Whether successes or failures in a persons life are attributed to oneself, (inner focus) or if you see that the reasons are some fated force outside of you. In other words as a result of events and the environment you live in, that affect you (external focus). In this case a sense of victimhood would persist. "

If a person has a high external locus of control he may continually find himself experiencing the same set of negative consequences over and over again; this occurs emotionally and also in terms of physical health.

An external focus of control looks at the environmental cultural factors, or the traditional status quo factors that tend to shape more fixed attitudes, which can only change with difficulty.

The way a person internalizes (inner focus) their understanding of control, directly determines their ability to live with a positive attitude. This again is a sentiment that others will more easily accept, encourage and agree with and ultimately vote for.

The reasons for this inner focus have a multitude of layers. First of all the individual themselves, their attitude and intellect, next the education and socialization of the parents, the mother is of particular significance, then the wider family have influence, also going back to grand parents and the social milieu that they lived in. Hence family background and history has an influence on who a person is.

So what we are saying is that Obama's grandfather, who was undoubtedly, influenced by Martin's visit to his tribe, also had an indirect influence on the first black President.

The subsequent introduction of Western schooling, which was encouraged by the Luo themselves and the way the Luo leaders helped in progressing the country to eventual independence, made it a positive environment for Obama's father to progress in school and then to study in the USA. No doubt Obama's white mother had so much to do with Barak's attitude. He also lived in more racially neutral countries, such as Hawaii and then the far East. Had he grown up in a Southern State of the United States, it is possible he would not have been so acceptable as a Presidential candidate. So he had a clear run, with few prejudicial hang-ups to slow him down.

Seen in this way, in 1883, at the starting blocks, the US black President candidate had a ball and chains tied to his ankle. There was no way he would win the race.

Instead an outsider from the Luo in Africa had that clear psychological advantage. It is a strategy that pays off in many areas of life, if you want to win or change something, bring in an outsider. He didn't carry the "negative history" and thus made himself electable by the American people as a whole. A positive agenda and can do attitude is the best way to win votes and keep the unity of the nation.

In an after thought to the Presidency, the electing and serving of a black President was certainly a milestone in world cultural acceptance, but it didn't solve or dissipate the prejudice that still exists in the society. It has certainly helped, but it didn't make America the racist free society some had dreamt of. That still has to be won.

11 First white hunter safari (1885–1886)

Once back in Zanzibar, Martin basked in the praise showered on him by Thomson. The Royal Geographical Society presented him with an inscribed gold watch for his work on the Thomson expedition, and his name surfaced whenever a new expedition within East Africa was mooted. Martin's services were all of a sudden in great demand. There were two types of clients that sought him out. One group were those interested in the basic logistics of transport caravans that were intended to carry supplies and generally increase trade and the influence of the British in the African interior (see next chapter). The other were wealthy people wanting to enjoy the adventure of hunting in Africa.

From this second category of clients came Sir John Willoughby, a captain in the Royal Horse Guards and a personal friend of the Prince of Wales, the future King Edward VII, who asked James to organise a safari. Willoughby had heard in London of James Martin's exploits with Joseph Thomson, and was convinced that

Martin was the best man to lead the private big game hunting expedition that he had decided to make in East Africa. His cabled enquiry (a cable station had been set up in Zanzibar only a few years before) was followed by his arrival by sea with his party. Martin suggested to him that the expedition should centre around Chagga country and the borders with Maasailand. He knew the area and the people well and could confirm that game of all sorts abounded. He also had his own base camp there. Because of the risks from the Maasai, Willoughby suggested for the supporting caravan an armed escort of sixty-five men, but on Martin's insistence this was increased by several more snider carbines and fifty muzzle-loaders. Captain Willoughby was clearly a wealthy customer and could afford the extra security. A large caravan on the march behind the British flag also fitted in with the official line (soon to be superseded) that stressed British supremacy in that disputed region. Martin himself was to have no fewer than five porters to carry his tent and personal baggage. Unusually, women bearers were included in the safari, though those with children were more of an encumbrance than a help. In fact during the expedition one wife went missing, which brought tension, accusations and fear to the group. Whether she got lost or was stolen was never known (cattle theft and theft of women often went hand in hand). Martin had to use all his skills of persuasion and discipline to stop this bad feeling from escalating. He swore never to bring women porters on an expedition again. There were also a number of slaves who were released temporarily by their masters on condition that they retained half their wages. So this was a mixed bag of people for Martin to manage as they had to live together for several months in difficult conditions. If fear gripped the porters, because of some unknown happening or a sign they read on the route, or the hostility of the locals, they might down their loads and vanish.

The expedition started off in November 1886 and in about a fortnight had reached the game area. The local chiefs were delighted to learn that Martin had returned and sent invitations for him to visit them. They each insisted that the expedition should pause in their own area. Doubtless they had an eye on the gifts and the trade that such a caravan brought with it. It was, of course, impossible to meet the wishes of all of them, and some, like Chief Mbugali, followed and caught up with Martin and complained, in a lengthy speech, that an old friend like Martin had passed by his place without stopping, even though a bullock had been killed in his honour. Martin proffered excuses and explained that the caravan was in a hurry to get to Taveta; he would call some other time.

At Taveta, Martin was able to guide the expedition to the compound and houses that he had constructed during his time with the Thomson expedition. Willoughby was impressed by the smart enclosure with its formidable thorn hedge and strong gateway. The square was enclosed on three sides, and on the fourth was a sparkling little river well stocked with fish. In the centre stood a tall pole, up which their flag was hoisted. Willoughby made it the base camp for their exploits. Martin went to see his friend and blood brother, the powerful Chief Mandara, and was given a great welcome. Other chiefs and elders greeted Martin and showed their friendship by refusing to claim any *chongo*, or transit charge, from Willoughby. This expression of friendship impressed Willoughby, who subsequently showered them with more gifts.

The game hunt, meanwhile, proceeded. It was hardly to Martin's liking, as although he approved of the shooting of game for food he did not like the indiscriminate killing of animals and was shocked by the massacre perpetrated by Willoughby's party. The final tally was over 350 beasts, 66 of them rhino, 40 zebra, 39 heartebeast, 39 umpala and 21 buffalo, plus smaller numbers of elephant, lion, leopard, giraffe and hippo. It is interesting to note that the rhino, with its phallic-looking horn, bore the brunt of the hunters' attention. This remains the case today, and these animals are continually fighting extinction as their horns are worth their weight in gold in modern eastern medicinal markets where they are sold as an aphrodisiac. Their actual medicinal value is, of course, zero.

Martin had to guard against a different set of risks in this safari: not the dangers of unexplored territory or unknown tribes but of wild animals. He had by this time picked up a lot of knowledge about game. Hunting for the pot was easy: impala, Thomson's gazelle and zebra were the preferred targets. It was just a question of getting close enough to the animal to get a good shot. Most times he was accompanied by a native tracker who could read the footprints and signs left by the animals. The golden rule in stalking was to make sure that you walked into the wind, so the game ahead would not get your scent and take flight. Having been a sailor, Martin was sensitive to picking up the wind direction and instinctively kept it in his mind at all times, even with just light breezes. Learning from the trackers, he also came to know the signs various animals left and how recent each track was. It was the bigger game that were more dangerous: lion, elephant, rhino and leopard, and most of all buffalo. But even these were not too difficult to hunt as the game only attacked if they were wounded or guarding their young. Usually they would take flight if they detected humans too close.

One day the hunting party were so successful tracking buffalo that they were able to creep up to a large herd, in savannah territory. They slowly moved forward, concealed by the long grass, taking their time to get a good shooting position for Willoughby. As he was about to take his shot, having singled out the largest horned buffalo, Martin, who was at his side, looked around him and to his surprise heard a grunt from behind. Turning round, he saw a group of buffalo where they had just come from. So they were encircled. The rear buffalos must have picked up the hunters' scent and done their own tracking to hunt them down.

'No, don't shoot!' Martin exclaimed, realising that, once they had fired a shot, the buffalos would stampede in all directions. In the ensuing chaos they would have little protection behind those small bushes. So instead they very slowly and quietly back-tracked through an opening in the herd and were lucky that the buffalos just stood and watched inquisitively, rather like a tame herd of cattle. Everyone knew that they could have charged at any moment. Outnumbered, the men felt totally at the mercy of these wild animals as they slowly slipped by them with bated breath, much sweating and rifles at the ready.

James still had in his mind the incident when Thomson was gored by a buffalo. Buffalo were here particularly dangerous again, and their tactics of ambushing were not forgotten. The wide horns across their heads also gave them a protective shield when they charged. The biggest problem in this messy, ugly business was when the game was wounded and had to be tracked down and killed. It was an unwritten rule to always go after wounded game and relieve them of their suffering. Martin would have insisted that all the 'guest hunters' practised their aim before the main hunt started, so as to have as few near-misses and wounded as possible. Once the game was shot, the native trackers would prepare the trophies for taxidermy treatment and mounting as a trophy. This in itself was a logistical problem, as the trophies had to be preserved in the right manner until they were treated; a taxidermist often accompanied the expedition. Seeing the graceful movements and beauty of the animals extinguished brought a feeling of regret to Martin, which more then cancelled out the initial excitement of the hunt.

On the way back, Captain Willoughby, leaving Martin at the camp, took the opportunity of climbing Mount Kilimanjaro. This must have been one of the first attempted ascents of the 19,000-foot volcano. It took four days to get to the top. The first day's trek was through an eerie forest full of mist with fungus trails hanging from the trees, some of which appeared to be dead. Once the party got above the forest, where the temperatures were now more akin to those of a northern European winter, a camp was made by a stream. The next day's march brought them onto higher ground above the treeline of the forests, from where they could clearly see the twin peaks of the snow-capped mountain. One peak was somewhat rugged and steep (Mawenzi); the other showed a gentler gradient and a large flat top (Kibo). The decision to climb the easier one was made with little discussion as it appeared to be the highest. They slept in caves on the second night and awoke to see the golden dawn sun rising above the thick blanket of white clouds below them. They were above the clouds. The third day was similar, with the slopes getting ever steeper. The final day was a much steeper climb, and several of the party had to turn back because of mountain sickness due to the lack of oxygen at that high altitude. It is, in fact, not clear how far up the mountain Willoughby climbed. It could have been that his party reached the top of the crater, which is not the summit of the mountain. (There is a long and treacherous walk around the snow-covered narrow rim of the large crater before reaching the top.) If he had reached the top he would have been the first person to have climbed Africa's highest peak. Three years later, Hans Meyer officially recorded the first full ascent, after two others had failed. He named the summit Kaiser Wilhelm Spitz.

On their return to the main party they met another big game safari on the move. This was led by Frederick Jackson and also had a large quantity of trophies. The two exchanged stories. The critical prize dimensions were the span of a buffalo's horns, the size of a lion's mane (black was preferable), the size and weight of an elephant's tusks, the size of a rhino's horn and the height of an antelope's horns (impala, water buck, eland or kudu). Each party would have boasted about the number and size of their 'bag'. On the conclusion of the expedition, Willoughby expressed his deep gratitude and indebtedness to Martin for his excellent services and gave him valuable commendations:

I can thoroughly recommend him to anyone contemplating an expedition in this country. Indeed I consider any traveller who does obtain his services exceptionally fortunate, and in the best possible position for conducting a successful and pleasurable trip.

Willoughby's big game hunting safari had lasted six months, until May 1887

The skills Martin developed of managing his clients to keep them safe and happy, while at the same time diplomatically 'controlling' their lust for trophies, was a new challenge and is one of the many skills required of a white hunter. The term was coined eight years later (1894) in a hunting expedition led by Lord Delemare, who referred to Alan Black as his 'White Hunter'. He is generally seen as the first professional white hunter in East Africa. Martin could, however, claim that distinction. It was to become a greatly sought-after profession in East Africa in the years ahead and the dream career for many a young lad. Martin had also witnessed one of the first attempted ascents of Kilimanjaro, an endeavour that would become a major tourist attraction in years to come.

12 Fixing boundaries and seeds of evil (1885 to 1986)

There were no borders when moving across Africa: there were just unclear demarcations between tribes. These were fluid owing to constant attacks that reduced villages, while other villages expanded and new villages were set up. The Maasai defined borders or boundaries in terms of where they moved in order to be able to graze their cattle. The rigid fixed border lines of Europe were unknown. Martin, on his return to Zanzibar, from both his last trip and also the Thomson trip, realised that there was added tension in the white population. Effectively, Africa had now been geographically discovered and it was the time to exert influence or colonise the land, to define limits and borders.

First Lloyd Mathews and then Sir John Kirk wanted to hear detailed accounts of Martin's long safari. They were particularly interested to debrief him, not only about the opening up of the route to the Great Lake, but as regards the attitude of the African chiefs towards strangers en route, and towards representatives of other large European powers bearing foreign flags. The Sultan also wished to hear Martin's account so that he could compare it with the various reports that had filtered through to him from his own subjects. To all, it confirmed that the tribes at the foothills of Mount Kilimanjaro were being stirred by the active German explorers and missionaries, notably Dr Carl Peters and Dr Juehlke. The Germans were concentrating on the areas south-east of Kilimanjaro. Although the British worked with the Sultan, the Germans were quite successful in securing contracts and agreements with the native tribes on their own. It was necessary to ensure that the influence of the Sultan (and therefore of Great Britain) did not suffer as a result.

The trouble was being stirred up by Dr Carl Peters, who within the course of two months had arrived in Zanzibar, gone across to the mainland and pressurised the African chiefs to opt for German overlordship. Dr Peters acted efficiently, fast and ruthlessly and was successful at what he did. Whoever first induced the local African chief to sign a declaration (which of course he could not read) was the victor. The chiefs were clearly perplexed, and at times signed agreements with both German and British representatives. One thing was clear: the British strategy of indirect influence was being usurped. Dr Peters hurried back to Germany with the agreements in his hand – which, on paper, and according to European legal frameworks, gave Germany an area of influence larger than Germany itself. He had acted more or less off his own bat, without the support of Bismarck's government. Peters made such a fuss in the press on getting back to Germany that Bismarck had, reluctantly, to support him and conveyed this authentication of the signed documents to the German Consul in Zanzibar.

British policy, which was to support and then dominate the Sultan's administration, was all at once in crisis. They had been caught sleeping and were out-manoeuvred. Lloyd Mathews decided to accelerate the build-up of the Sultan's military forces. He was given the rank of

Brigadier General, mainly to impress the African chiefs on the mainland and so that he would have adequate rank and standing to deal with German officials. He engaged Martin as his second-in-command with the rank of Colonel. (Martin never used the title, and to the men remained 'Bwana Martini'.) The regular force soon numbered 1,400, and General Mathews could call upon a couple of thousand irregulars if they were needed. The arms and drill training was done by Nubian or Sudanese non-commissioned officers, and Martin, who knew very little of military matters, exercised a general supervisory role, particularly in the quartermaster's department. Once a week, on Fridays, resplendent in the uniform specially concocted for him – a tunic laden with lots of gold braid, loose white trousers and a gold-handled curved sword, the whole surmounted by a large pith helmet bearing an imposing brass badge of the Sultan's Army (a uniform resembling the carnival costumes of his youth) – Martin reviewed the troops with General Mathews outside the Old Portuguese Fort near the Sultan's Palace. This was the Beit el-Ajaib, or

House of Wonders, so named because of its unusual Victorian style of construction, with wide encircling wooden verandas carried on slender iron pillars.

On 16 June 1885, General Mathews, with Martin and 200 soldiers, crossed over to the mainland on a twelve-day military expedition to the country around Mount Kilimanjaro. The purpose of the expedition was ostensibly to meet the request of Chief Mandara, made via Martin when he was there with Thomson's expedition, to be placed under the protection of the Sultan of Zanzibar. But it was also intended to fly the British flag and find out what damage Dr Peters had done. The Germans sent five gunships to patrol the area. An arms race between Britain and Germany had begun, as had the fight, or scramble, for the domination and exploitation of the now discovered East Africa, which according to the explorers would be lucrative. The war of words was mainly between Britain, Germany and the Sultan, who tried to play his own game.

Martin would probably have met Dr Carl Peters, and although both were of similar short height their characters were poles apart. Peters's character was having an impact. A complex man, he had obtained his doctoral degree from Berlin having written a thesis on the philosopher Schopenhauer – who among other things in his writings attributed 'civilisation to primarily the northern white races'. Peters went out to Zanzibar and the mainland in 1884. After returning to Germany with his agreements, he formed the Society for German Colonisation, which in 1887 was taken over and renamed by Bismarck as the German East Africa Company. Peters was put in charge as administrator, with the right to a coveted German pension. He was brutal and ruthless, and acted on his ideas on white supremacy to which he gave full rein – quite unlike the many good German missionaries who now moved into mainland Africa through Bagamoya.

Pressure back in Europe meant that Britain had no stomach for any conflict in the African colonies, and Lord Granville and Otto von Bismarck were eager to manage the situation and stop it escalating. France, Britain and Germany set up a commission whose report provided the basis of the Anglo-German Agreement of 1886. The mainland was divided by a straight line running from Lake Victoria, north of Kilimanjaro, to Vanga, just north of Tanga on the east coast. (The Witu area would be given up to Britain by Germany; the Sultan was accorded a ten-mile strip of the coast.) A close look at the two straight lines of the 1,000-mile partition showed that Taveta, where James had his camp (the land was purchased from the chief), was in the German sphere by just a couple of miles. Obviously, protests were raised by the Sultan and perhaps by Martin himself. This resulted in the straight and rigid British and Prussian lines being modified by a small irregular blip indentation that pushed Taveta – Martin's camp – and part of Lake Jipe into the British sphere. Seeing this irregularity that kept his camp British must have brought a smile to Martin's face every time he looked at the map of the Kenya–Tanganyika border, which is still the same in today's maps. It must also have caused raised eyebrows in the capitals of Europe which were trying to clean up the whole situation. It was visible enough to annoy the methodical, high-powered European dignitaries gathered around the treaty table in Berlin, but not large enough to raise a complaint. Perhaps the blip, Martin's blip, in the border was a cry of protest from Africa. The illogical irregularity of the boundary notch would be questioned in times to come, but it is only in an understanding of Martin's times that we will find the answer. The partition gave more clarity between Britain and Germany, but muddied the waters for the Sultan and the Coast Arabs who now had to accommodate the Germans instead of the British. Dr Peters, now in charge, was not making it easy.

Peters didn't last long in his position as German High Commissioner. It leaked out from the missionaries that he kept a concubine, and when one of his lovers had an affair with his man-servant, he had them both tried for theft and treason by a quasi-court martial and went on to have them hanged and their villages burnt down. Bismarck's Reichstag dismissed Peters immediately, and he forfeited his pension. He remained in Africa, going first to Uganda and then to other parts of the continent. Later he returned to Germany and also lived in England for a while. He wrote about and published his ideas and the stories of his exploits in Africa, gaining a following with extreme right-wing circles in Germany: after all, he had provided Germany with a doubling of their much wanted 'lebensraum'. As if to magnify the notoriety of his deeds, after his death he was fully rehabilitated by the German government under Adolf Hitler. He was hailed as a hero, and a propaganda film was even made about him. The philosophy that inspired the building of Auschwitz, one of contempt, hatred, brutality and disrespect, was given its first dark wings of flight in the vulnerable people "administered" by Peters.

13 Race for Uganda (1889–94)

On returning from his campaign with General Mathews, James Martin was again called upon to furnish and direct a porterage caravan for an eight-month safari by Sir Robert Harvey, with whom he had already travelled up the Tana river. This expedition was moving westward. He thus became more involved with caravans towards Uganda and probably never set foot in Traveta again using the old route which was now in the German sphere. In his travels and visits to Zanzibar, James Martin would have heard the many stories and legends of the Uganda area. The Kingdom of Buganda (part of Uganda) stands at the north-west corner of Victoria Nyanza. Until the end of the nineteenth century it was accessible to strangers only if they approached up the west side of the Great Lake, which meant a long and unenticing journey from the coast. An approach from Sudan meant traversing the impassable Sudd, and negotiating hostile country. There also existed a traditional belief that the first white man to enter

Buganda from the east would overthrow the Kabakaship. Thus the Baganda for centuries had lived in splendid isolation. The curious thing is that they alone in East and Central Africa had developed an advanced system of government, with a king and a royal court, ministers, a parliament, and a hierarchy of local and subordinate chiefs. The king, or Kabaka, was absolutely ruthless and enforced his will without concern for human life. On his accession, every male relative in the kingdom who could in any way be considered to have the least possible claim to the throne was mercilessly murdered and thrown to the crocodiles in the lake outside the Kabaka's palace. In this way it was ensured that there were never any pretenders to the throne. Individuals, men or women, were shot or mutilated at his whim for petty indiscretions such as not wearing the correct dress or for speaking out of turn or giggling in court. When Speke, on his first visit to Buganda, presented a gift of rifles and guns to Kabaka Mutesa and explained their operation, the Kabaka selected one of the weapons, loaded it, and handing it full cock to an aide told him to go outside and shoot a man 'to see how it worked'. The order was obeyed without hesitation and without a thought for the victim.

The first recorded visit of a caravan to Buganda was that of some Arab traders in 1840. Next, in 1862, the explorers James Grant and John Hanning Speke, looking for the elusive source of the Nile, entered Buganda from the west and were detained for some months by the Kabaka before Speke discovered the source of the Nile at a cataract (the Ripon Falls) at the northern end of Lake Victoria. Here, a large volume of water flowed out in unrestrained confusion on the start of its 4,000-mile journey to the Mediterranean: on 28 July 1862 the mystery that had exercised the minds of the civilised world for so long was solved. (The famous Bernini fountain in Piazza Navona in Rome, representing the four great rivers of the world, shows a representation of the Nile as an African with his head hidden under a cloak.) Anglican missionaries in 1877 and the White Fathers of Cardinal Lavigerie's missionary order in 1879 reached Buganda, again from the west, but the first attempt to enter the Buganda kingdom from the east (the 'back door') met with disaster. On the express order of the Kabaka of Baganda an entire caravan, with Bishop James Hannington and his CMS missionaries, was massacred as it approached the Nile – a seemingly senseless slaughter and act of barbarity.

What the missionaries didn't understand was that the Baganda had been in a long-term rivalry with their western neighbours, the Banyoro: both had dominated from time to time; both had large organised armies, similarly structured. Hence if the Kabaka perceived any threat to enter his territory, particularly from his back door, he treated it very seriously. He had had previous experience of weapons being supplied to his rivals, and they all came from the east. Hence he tried to keep this back door, the eastern approach, guarded. He had the upper hand at this point and would not have wanted his neighbour to get an advantage that could tip the balance of power – particularly if he was led to believe that these were strangers with 'some unknown spiritual powers' who didn't even have to carry weapons to protect themselves: hence a possible explanation for this savage and unjustified reaction. It was, however, a grave misfortune, which highlighted the mistrust that existed.

The pace of opening up what remained of unallocated Africa could not, however, be slowed. With the future Tanzania and Kenya now partitioned between Germany and Great Britain, there developed a race for mastery of Buganda. While the great powers in their European capitals continued to haggle and discuss, in Africa they operated surreptitiously through 'imperial' trading companies such as the Imperial British East Africa Company (IBEA) and the German East Africa Company (GEA). These companies did indeed engage in trade, but they were probably more interested in furthering the expansionist ideas of their fatherlands, often going beyond the orders or the intentions of their respective governments.

In 1889, the IBEA Company appointed Frederick Jackson and Ernest

Gedge to undertake a prolonged safari to survey, map and set up posts along the route to Uganda, and thus the infrastructure to be able secure it and make the necessary treaties. At the same time, unbeknown to them, Dr Carl Peters set off on his own safari aiming to be the first to establish the Kaiser's influence over Kabaka Mutesa in Buganda. Dr Peters's caravan was not properly financed or organised (it did not have full German recognition). He marched up along the Tana river, brooking no interference and dealing savagely with any opposition. In Kikuyuland he shot six Africans who slowed his progress. This was Prussian ruthlessness at its worst: his goal was Uganda. Frederick Jackson's caravan, on the other hand, was organised with proper care and attention to detail. The IBEA was responsible for all arrangements, and the obvious choice for the leader of this large and well-equipped caravan could only be James Martin, who by then had joined the IBEA Company. With Gedge he went to Zanzibar and chose his Zanzibari porters and askaris, many of whom had travelled with him on earlier safaris. Stores and equipment were purchased and a return made to Mombasa in time for the caravan to leave on 18 June 1889. Jackson remained behind, but caught up and joined the party a month later at Machakos. The caravan, over 500 strong and well armed, moved on for the next eight months in the country of the Maasai, the Kikuyu and the Nandi, avoiding warriors on the warpath and areas where tribal battles were being fought, but at times having to fight through tribal opposition. It is recorded that in this period Martin cut off his thick beard but kept his moustache, that Gedge and Jackson tried unsuccessfully to teach him to write, and that Martin kept tally of the men, loads and equipment under his charge by drawing a series of lines and hooks and his own concoction of hieroglyphs that his dyslexic mind could read.

One thing the 1886 partition between German and British East Africa meant was that the usual caravan route to the interior, which used to go inland from Tanga and round the south of Kilimanjaro (as Thomson had done earlier), was now in German East Africa, so the caravan had to proceed inland from Mombasa higher up the coast. A route through the Kenya region existed and was used by Arab and Swahili expeditions in search of slaves and ivory; however, this route went through the dreaded Taru desert. The details of the hardships of Martin's trek with Gedge can only be understood by looking at the detail. It was along a narrow track of about 700 miles fraught with danger. All the luggage had to be carried by porters. Animals such as donkeys could not be used because of the tsetse fly, which infected and killed them. Each porter carried a load weighing up to 60 pounds for ten to fifteen miles a day. It was best to avoid the rainy seasons – either the short rains in October to November or the long rains in March to May. Starting out from Mombasa and heading north-west the terrain was pleasant, with moderate temperatures tempered by the sea, although the high humidity could be oppressive. Vegetation included coconut trees, tamarind, oranges, bananas and mangoes. The first fifteen miles, or the first day's travel, were easy. The stop at Mariakindi marked the start of the Taru desert with its waterless terrain and red dust, sparse acacia and a few strange baobab trees.

The fifty-five-mile desert took three days to cross. The expedition's goal was to reach Maungu, which was the next safe water stop. All their water had to be carried by the porters along with their full loads. Without shade, the going was relentless. The heavy, precious water partly evaporated or was lost or even stolen along the way.

To cross this wilderness the caravans had worked out a method called *terekeza*, or 'two marches a day'. The first day, from Mariakani to Taru, was done in two walks with a break between. The food they ate was mainly locally grown fruit, such as mangoes and bananas. The second day's march started from Taru at dawn with the remaining water and food. They stopped at Buchuma for a rest and a drink. The caravan then pushed through until dark, when they stopped but without taking any food or water. Just before daylight on the final day, having eaten and drunk what remained, they pressed on with the objective of reaching Maungu hill. This they had to reach without water or food, so it was vital that they got there before nightfall, or they would probably die. The climb up the hill to reach the water that lay in a depression was a final challenge.[11] A successful crossing of the desert required detailed logistical planning and total discipline from all.

Most desertions of porters occurred in the early stages of the desert; roaming alone in this hostile environment usually led to death by dehydration. It was reported that Martin used to tie the porters together until they were far enough into the desert to prevent them from running away and perishing. The caravan was only as fast as its weakest link. Many men got sick and died. Disease claimed many (smallpox and malaria were common); attacks by animals (among them hyena and lion) claimed other lives. Sickness caused delay. It was not an uncommon occurrence, after two or so miles of a day's journey, for a porter to break down. When this happened, the line of men was ordered to halt, a litter constructed, and five men's loads distributed among the other porters, an action likely to produce near rebellion (though the sick man's pay was distributed among them to prevent malingering). If the porter was desperately ill and water was far away, the caravan was split in two and the advance party and invalid travelled at full speed to the source with the white man in attendance. After water was reached, the invalid and a few porters would stay while the European and the other men returned to the rest of the caravan with water for those left behind.[12]

It was only when the caravan reached the Voi river (a hundred miles from the coast) and the Taita hills that the worst part of the journey was over and regular good water could be found along the way. The country was now open savannah with plenty of game. Impala and gazelle provided the main diet and vitamins at this stage. Among other problems that affected the expedition was hostility from the local tribes through whose territory the caravan passed. If discipline was lacking, some of the porters would steal crops or molest local women. The reaction could be severe, with attacks on the caravan. Communication with local chiefs was the key and Martin was good at this. Negotiations agreed on a 'transit fee' that would compensate for such incidents. The caravan head porter, or *kilangozi*, would mete out to the culprits appropriate punishments that might appear drastic in today's world, but docking of pay or flogging or chain gang duty was the law of the time.

The next major stopping point was Kibwezi, which was an eight-day trek. Along the way the expedition halted at Tsavo and Mtito Andei. Each stopping point presented its own trial for getting water. In places they had to dig into the often dried-up river bed to access the water below. Some pools were covered in weeds. It was always an act of faith that the water at the next stop would be all right. There was the added danger in this sector of lions attacking the porters at night. A ring of thorn bushes around the camp was necessary for additional protection.

On the twenty-sixth day of the trek they arrived at Machakos. The friendly chief was known to welcome travellers, and it was one of the first posts that traded with the visitors. Jackson heard on arriving that the leader had unfortunately died the previous year, but his name, Machako, lived on. This was one of the larger posts at that time.

The next major stop was Ngong Bagas – now called Ngong – in Kikuyuland (near the area where Karen Blixen had her farm many years later). By this stage the party had been trekking for thirty days. The Kikuyu cultivated their land and were good trading partners so the caravan stocked up with fruit, vegetables and meat (from cattle and chickens). This had to last them until the next main food station at Mumias, which was three weeks away. The journey climbed higher through the red-coloured, richly vegetated Kikuyuland, with its large forests. In contrast to the Taru desert, where temperatures reached 40°C, the highlands were often frosty with 0°C temperatures at night – a further challenge to the logistics of providing adequate clothing for each stage of the journey.

The Rift Valley was the next big event. They travelled along its ridge for a while, then descended 600 metres via the Kedong valley. Once on the flat valley floor they passed the prominent volcano Longonot on their left and proceeded to the beautiful Lake Naivasha. This part of the journey was again easy going, with moderate temperatures and flat land. The caravan was by now 400 miles and thirty-four days into its journey, with another 220 miles to go to get to Mumias. The lake could be passed on the south-west side if the river on the east side happened to be flooded. The land provided meat in the form of impala and gazelles, which were abundant there. They carried on towards Lake Nakuru: its covering of thousands of pink flamingos must have been uplifting for any traveller. The caravan then had a three-day climb up the other side of the Rift Valley. The journey through the Mau hills and their forests took another seven days. The Mau summit was a climb up to 3,000 metres, and again temperatures could get cold at night.

After this came the obstacle of the thick tropical rain forest, thought to be one of the most hostile and impenetrable environments on earth, its tall straight trees creating a canopy that cut out much of the sunlight. There was, however, less undergrowth here because of the diminished light, and this facilitated walking. The air was humid and a potential carrier of disease. There was also a heightened danger of a different set of wild creatures, especially snakes including the giant python, which grows up to twenty feet long and catches, crushes and kills smaller animals before swallowing them whole. (These snakes are fearsome to behold but in fact move so slowly that they are less of a danger to humans than the smaller poisonous varieties.) The pathway in the forest was often obscured, which increased the travellers' uncertainty.

Eventually they arrived at Mumias (or Kwi Sundu) in the region so-uth-east of Mount Elgon. The arrival of a caravan in Mumias was a special event, and it marked the end of the journey for most. Some of the porters would be dressed in their leopard skins and ostrich feathers, and a band of drummers would welcome the party into the camp. The Lake Victoria shores were rife with malaria, and Europeans were highly susceptible. At night clouds of mosquitoes hid the moon and the mosquito nets that were so vital at the coast were used again in this area. At this point the caravan was fifty-one days from the coast. Probably several of the porters would have died by this time. In all, the Uganda caravan had been on foot for two and a half months, and once they had rested it would take them the same amount of time to return to the coast. The men on a caravan were away from their homes and family for between five and six months. Europeans saw their arrival back in Mombasa as a return to civilisation.

This was James Martin's daily life, and it was no mean undertaking. He had to manage the porters of different tribes, see that they were all up in time in the mornings, provide food, look after the sick, stop porters deserting, limit the thieving, and keep track of the numerous goods and supplies they carried. No wonder that so few people had ventured into the interior, and that Kenya and Uganda had remained cut off from the rest of the world for so long. When diseases like dysentery struck a caravan, porters could die by the dozen. The head porter had an important role, not only as regards discipline but also in terms of morale. One thing he would do when the trek was on a flat run would be to sing out a loud safari chant in a high voice

'Funga Safarii! Quenda Mariakanii!'
The several hundred porters of different tribes would reply, with a loud and perfect pitch and timing:
'Eheee!

It was awesome, and reflected the combined power of the caravan: a moment only Africa could bring. The head porter carried on and improvised on the content of the chant, often making comments about their difficulties or even about the white leader of the trek. Some comments were quite humorous and brought a smile to the porters' faces that the white leader himself never quite understood. There were many Swahili safari songs:

'*Pesi pesi, pesa, pesa!*' (Quick quick, money, money!) or - '*Upesi, upesi, hata Baringo – mbale kidogo, tutafika Buganda!*' (Hurry, hurry, we've reached Baringo – it's only a short distance to Buganda)

Jackson's caravan eventually reached Kavirondo, the nearest region to Buganda, and there found letters written months before, with an invitation from the Kabaka and the White Father missionaries in Rubaga for him to hasten to place Buganda under British protection. Dr Peters had been there earlier, had opened the letter addressed to Jackson and had hurried post haste to the Kabaka and persuaded him, less than a month before, to sign a treaty of allegiance with Germany. Dr Peters had done it again and beaten the British to their goal. Jackson was too late, and was naturally upset and disappointed that he had lost the race, no doubt wondering whether Uganda would now go the same way as the Kilimanjaro region and become part of the German-sphere.

Jackson remained in Kampala for only a

month – just enough time to rest and visit the CMS and the Catholic missions, and to receive a return call from them – and then, feeling rather dejected his caravan, led by Martin, started the return journey to Mombasa with news of the German achievement. The safari back took three and a half months and reached Mombasa on 4 September 1890. However, as fate would have it, during the course of the journey the political situation in respect of Uganda had changed completely. The highest representatives of the two European powers, regardless of what was happening in Africa, came to a mutually acceptable agreement whereby Great Britain handed over to Germany the small island of Heligoland situated in the North Sea off the German coast, and in return was given sovereignty over the African countries of Uganda and Equatoria and the small kingdom of Witu on the coast. In addition, Germany recognised Zanzibar as a British Protectorate. Dr Carl Peters had hardly been given time to announce his achievement before it was denounced by his government in the Anglo-German treaty of 1890. Jackson's annoyance turned to euphoria on hearing the news when they got back to Mombasa.

Again, what was happening in East Africa in Martin's time meant that the British were occupied in the colonial scramble for Africa, and at this stage they wanted to secure Uganda and negate Dr Peter's agreements. They were distracted from the real importance of the situation in their backyard – Europe – and bargained away Heligoland: one of the many contributory factors that led to start of the First World War: another thread of history woven from Africa. (Heligoland, just outside the main port of Hamburg, effectively could control a major part of German shipping, hence with the island theirs, they could now build a naval fleet to rival,Britain's)

As Jackson's caravan made its way to Mombasa, another caravan, fitted out by the Imperial British East Africa Company and commanded by Captain F. Lugard, was moving westwards to build stations at Ngong and Dagoretti and then await instructions. When these instructions arrived, they were to proceed forthwith to Buganda and there undertake the administration of the newly acquired country. Lugard arrived on Christmas Day 1890 and the next day made a treaty with Kabaka Mwanga. The bringing of Buganda under the control of the Imperial British East Africa Company meant that supplies of all kinds would have to be sent regularly from Mombasa. Until the railway was built, there was only one way to solve this problem: the traditional foot safari, with ever increasing numbers of porters.

James Martin's worth and his position in the company as chief transport officer became more significant, and for the next few years he led important safari caravans to and from Uganda, a distance of 800 miles each way, on average at least twice a year. He had tremendous stamina, and seemed immune to the illnesses that beset travellers in the bush as a result of insects, wild beasts, poor diet and fatigue. The safari marches wound their way from camp site to camp site, or from post to post, these stopping-points often bearing the names of local leaders or chiefs. Some were well-built stockaded forts, like Dagoretti and Fort Smith; others were merely a clearing with a cluster of huts, like Mumias or Lubas, which helped to relieve the hardships of the caravans by supplying water and locally grown vegetables or trading tea and small essential goods. As he repeatedly traversed the distance, he sought to improve and shorten the route. With him lies the credit for discovering the more direct and shorter route to Uganda through Uasin-Ghisu.

Martin's first Uganda supply convoy left Mombasa on 8 December 1890 laden with stores, arms and ammunition for Captain Lugard. The 800-mile journey lasted three and a half months, and when it arrived the caravan was in a bad way, with several porters suffering from sores and ulcers. Lugard was shocked. He blamed Martin, and complained to the company that it had not allowed sufficient finance for the expedition to be properly prepared and conducted. These hard marches could be brutally harsh, and often needed pure discipline to move them forward. While this narrative errs on the positive side of James Martin, his arduous task must have also brought out a darker side.

Without much of a respite Martin marched back to Mombasa, leaving Kampala in April; but he was back in Kampala on 9 December bringing, besides a large supply of arms and ammunition, two horses and a pony and a steel boat in sections that weighed seventy pounds. When assembled the vessel was 24 feet long and was named the *James Martin.* (Later, in 1907, it was part of the flotilla used to convey Winston Churchill on his journey down the Nile from the foot of the Murchison Falls to Lake Albert and on to Nimule in Sudan.) With Martin on his return safari to the coast in January 1892 went some 300 of Emin Pasha's Sudanese evacuees, who had been cut off by the Mahdi rebellion in Sudan and were taking the long way back home via Mombasa, the Red Sea and Egypt.

The origins of the Sudanese troops in Uganda, whose descendants still form the backbone of the various branches of the African Rifle regiments in East Africa, go back to the time of the Mahdi's massacre of the British garrison under General Gordon in Khartoum in 1885. The Mahdi's victory cut off Equatoria from the north of Sudan and with it the Governor of Equatoria, Emin Pasha, and his garrison of around 10,000 Egyptians and Sudanese, which included a large following of women and children. Unable to travel towards Khartoum and with the way south along the River Nile blocked by the swampy and almost impenetrable Sudd, Emin Pasha and his army were 'lost'. An Emin Pasha Relief Committee was set up to finance and organise an expedition to find and rescue Emin. Joseph Thomson (who with James Martin had travelled through Maasailand in 1883) was first suggested as its leader, but the final choice fell on Henry Morton Stanley. Stanley, ever hungry for publicity and fame, mounted a formidable expedition from the west coast of Africa through Congo.

In the event, however, Emin Pasha and his army did not need rescuing. The party gradually travelled down from Sudan to Wadelai and into Uganda. While Emin Pasha – who although employed by General Gordon had been born in the Prussian province of Silesia – went off to join the Germans in German East Africa, his Sudanese followers settled down in Uganda for good. The Arab soldiers were the only trained military men in Central Africa, and from them the British newcomers to Uganda recruited their security forces and military units. These Sudanese troops were to give James Martin his first real headache at his new posting at Eldama Ravine, because it was near there that in September 1897 several hundred Sudanese troops started a revolt which spread as further garrisons mutinied. Three British officers had been murdered and numerous askaris had lost their lives before it was quelled. Stanley arrived in Zanzibar in February 1887 at the start of his expedition to find Emin Pasha, while Martin was on a safari with Willoughby. Following the conclusion of his quest, Stanley left Zanzibar for the last time on 29 December 1889, while Martin was on his Uganda trek with Gredge and Jackson. Thus Martin never had the chance to meet one of the great explorers of the age, who had also spoken Swahili.

Over the next years, until 1894, Martin conducted large caravans to and from Uganda with amazing regularity (see Appendix 2). He became a well-known and popular figure on the safari that became more or less established along this regular route. He was allowed by the IBEA Company to undertake trading on his own account, and according to reports was at this time making a profit of between £2,000 and £3,000 a year, mainly by trading ivory from elephant tusks. He accompanied all the well-known leaders and administrators who travelled to Uganda – Lord Lugard, Sir Frederick Jackson, Major J. R. MacDonald, Sir Gerald Portal and many others – and won their friendship on the three-month safari. He conveyed mail to Uganda and back, and with it his own verbal reports of historic political events that were unfolding in his path.

Some amusing anecdotes have been written about Martin at this time. Once at Tsavo river, hot and exhausted, the caravan porters stripped naked and plunged into the water. Martin was about to follow their example but saw some nude native women watching him with curiosity. He refused to undress in their presence and although much in need of a bath preferred to wait until darkness fell before taking his turn. On another occasion, while he was traversing Maasai country with MacDonald, they were confronted by a group of spear-waving Maasai Moran, who insisted at all costs that MacDonald should give them some potent medicine to ensure protection and invincibility in battle. Not being able to satisfy their wishes, MacDonald was about to have them dispersed when Martin asked to be allowed to deal with the Maasai himself. Taking a bottle of Eno's Fruit Salts, he moved the Maasai a short distance away and, with some ceremony, poured water into tumblers to which he added a pinch of the effervescent powder. The strange bubbling of the water made them laugh, encouraged by Martin. The effect on the Maasai of swallowing this cold 'boiling' medicine was impressive. They felt they were now impregnable, and readily rewarded Martin with four donkeys for his trouble. Martin explained to the amused MacDonald that he had not fooled them entirely since the Eno's salts could not but have a salutary effect on their bodies and thus make them fitter warriors! Everyone left with a smile.

14 Administrator of the land, (1894–1904)

In June 1894, the British government took over the responsibilities, the obligations and the staff of the British East Africa Company, including James Martin, who suddenly found himself appointed a District Officer in the Uganda Administration. The new Uganda Protectorate extended its boundaries from the Mountains of the Moon in the west as far as Lake Naivasha in the east, in territory that is now part of Kenya. Its easternmost outpost was the stockaded camp of the District of Eldama at Ravine, forty-seven miles north of Nakuru. Martin was put in charge of Ravine Station and arrived there on 7 January 1895.

The area around Ravine and the safari trails leading to the station from Dagoretti in Kenya and from Mumias in the north were beset by raiding warriors of the fearsome Maasai and Nandi tribes, who when not fighting each other or other tribes attacked supply caravans, stealing loads and killing people. The trail being so vulnerable, the District Officer at Ravine had to provide armed escorts to the next post for the ever increasing number of private caravans run by missionaries and traders. The Nandi were particularly active in the area and had shortly before killed a British officer. Delay in mounting an armed expedition to punish the murderers merely encouraged them to be more audacious and arrogant, and reports came through to Martin that they were planning to attack Ravine. He at once set himself to reinforce the perimeter stockade, asked for reinforcements of askaris from other districts, and strove to build up his stores of food, arms and ammunition. He also asked for increased rations, and for trade goods such as beads and cloth to enable him to purchase more food locally: he believed in beads rather than bullets for solving disputes. The next station, Mumias, was depleted of men in order to help Ravine be properly defended.

Martin was no trained soldier, but he knew the country and habit of the people around him, and above all he was well informed. Because of his illiteracy, he privately employed a Goanese clerk, Anacleto de Silva, to do all his paperwork and to write his reports and letters, which he could now at least sign. He welcomed the change from the restless life he had been living, and discovered the joy and comfort of having his own bungalow furnished with all conveniences, many of which he had paid for himself. He could grow and pick his own vegetables and arrange things as he wanted. He extended warm hospitality to visitors, of whom there were quite a few as Ravine was an important staging post. In order to administer the area he got to know the various tribes, their languages and customs better. This enabled him to be a fair administrator who understood the concerns of the people.

15 Setting up family, home and city (1896)

Having now been in charge of Eldama Ravine for twelve months, James Martin found that he was a lot better off than he used to be. His part-time trading in ivory and beads had helped him build up his finances. He had been living in one fixed place now for a longer period than he had for years, and he used this time to make his bungalow into a home. He wanted to build on this stability. He was now thirty-six years old and believed that it was time to start a family: it was now or never. Out on the treks he had always had something to do. Being in a fixed place, he felt lonelier than he ever had done before. Since 1985 Eldama Ravine and Fort Smith had grown rapidly as a result of the increase in traffic to the interior. It was estimated by Francis Hall that from 1,500 to 2,000 people would travel through on their way to Uganda between September and November 1894.[13] Martin was now well-known throughout the country and was proud of the position he had established for himself. He decided to go on leave back to the more civilised coast and get married. He set off on 27 December 1895 for Mombasa and then, after selling some of the goods he had brought with him, went to meet his old friends in Zanzibar.In his many travels, he always visited his doctor on his return to Zanzibar, if not to get treatment for himself or to stock up on medicine then to gather advice about the sickness of one or other of his bearers. He tried to understand the causes of any deaths and to take necessary precautions for the future. So he was slowly turning into a basic medical treatment expert and made sure he knew the remedy for each common illness. He effectively had to act as the doctor when any of his caravan became ill and must have built up his medical knowledge together with an understanding of the use of local remedies. His consultations with the doctor often became more like social chats over a shared meal. The doctor was interested in all things to do with the interior. Martin's 'nursing' of Thomson in his long illness had taught him a lot, and made him keen to seek further knowledge. So there was a genuine mutual friendship between himself and the doctor now.

Martin couldn't help noticing the doctor's daughter on his visits. She was a bit younger than him, and slightly shorter (Martin being a relatively short man compared to the people around him). She had a slender figure and sharp delicate features, and a darkish Mediterranean complexion with large dark eyes, not unlike those of some of the pretty girls back in Malta. She was jovial, and Martin and her found it easy to crack jokes and laugh with her. So one thing led to another and a relationship gradually built up over the years. This was one reason that he always tried to get back to Zanzibar, and this time he came not as a wandering traveller with no fixed abode, but as a man who had an established position and a nice house that needed looking after. He had also brought plenty of gifts.

Everything went as he had hoped and while there he married, on 9 April 1896, the pretty petite Portuguese Maria Augusta Elvira de Souza, daughter of this respected Zanzibar doctor. They were married by the

British Agent and Consul, General A. H. Harding, and the witnesses were Arthur E. Raikes and Martin's old friend General Sir Lloyd Mathews. Martin's marriage certificate describes him as 'Transport Officer, Uganda, aged 36 years – son of Antonio Martini, a 3rd Officer in the Mercantile Marine'. Martin took his time with a long honeymoon of several months' duration. He felt he had earned it, and the companionship of married life suited him well. Part of the honeymoon was spent on the relaxing coast of Mombasa, with its white sandy beaches and coconut trees almost dipping into the sea.

While in Mombasa, Martin met George Whitehouse, the chief engineer in charge of constructing the railway, who had arrived a few months earlier. Whitehouse had asked him to set up a camp upcountry to recruit Africans for the construction of the railway. According to the studies carried out and Martin's advice, a central camp in the Kikuyuland would be the best option for both climatic and personnel reasons. This started Martin's association with – and, on and off, work on – the construction of the railway. He collected the required materials for the camp and took them up with him, along with his bride. He made special arrangements for Elvira to ride in state: she had a special seat with a roof and was carried by two bearers. Elvira must have felt like a queen as she proceeded into the African unknown.

When Martin reached Kikuyuland he selected the flat spot that he thought best for his camp. It was near a water source – the Nairobi river was close by – and just below a hill (later to be known as Nairobi Hill). When the tents were put up and all the basics completed, he left some of his askaris to guard the camp and continued on to Fort Smith to show Elvira the next station, at which they arrived on 20 September 1896. Martin in true fashion arranged celebrations, inviting all his friends so that they could be introduced to his new bride. There was quite a gathering: James Wallace and his wife Mary came to Fort Smith, as did two other married couples, Henry and Helen Boedeker and James and Mary McQueen. Both Mrs Wallace and Mrs McQueen were pregnant.[14] Martin had also arranged for his bride to officially open the Ngong Fort that same month, so they travelled down, probably with the other couples. Elvira, dressed in her smart Victorian dress, hoisted the flag 'to the sound of two bugles frightfully out of tune'.[15] The fort was named Fort Elvira in her honour. Martin had made a great effort to make her feel that she belonged upcountry.

Also in September 1896, an Edward Russell went to 'Nairobi' to see 'Mr Martin and his new bride'.[16] This is the first mention of Nairobi as a place. East African maps prior to 1897 show two sites indicated as 'Martin's Camp', one of them being on the spot where the future Nairobi railway station was established, and the future capital of Kenya. It was a little later that Elvira became pregnant, and after long discussions they felt it would be better if she returned to Zanzibar to have her baby. A recent Maasai raid on a caravan in the Kedong valley had killed over 600 African porters;[17] this unrest must have added weight to the decision for her to return to Zanzibar in early 1897. James, meanwhile, had to get on with the work of improving the camp for the railways.

It seems a fitting coincidence that Martin, who was the known expert in leading the way into Kenya and Uganda and had already done much to open them up, was entrusted with the development of the camp that was to become Nairobi. It is also interesting that it was not part of an existing African/Kikuyu village. Nairobi owed its early success to being the centre and headquarters of the railway, halfway between the coast and Uganda. It then developed into an all-tribe centre, not belonging to any traditional group, and people from all areas were tempted into the city to seek the peace and safety that they did not have at home. It became a melting pot for inter-tribal friendship and was a refuge for those who had escaped conflicts and sought the promise of opportunity. It grew rapidly and symbolised the new colonial era more then any other place. Although there exists a street named after James Martin in Kampala, Uganda, there is nothing in Nairobi to indicate the city's earliest origins.

The years 1896–7 had been a rollercoaster for Martin's emotions. He had achieved so much and fulfilled his dream of getting married. It was hard for him when his wife went back to the coast and he had to carry on with his job. His friends Mrs Wallace and Mrs McQueen both gave birth to their children upcountry – only the second and third white babies to be born there. Henry Boedeker was a doctor, so it is quite probable that he assisted at the births. (The first white baby to have been born away from the coast was J. A. Stuart Watt, at Negelani on 23 August 1895.)

Elvira gave birth in Zanzibar to her first child, a daughter, whom they named Magdalene. Unfortunately, in spite of the efforts of Elvira's father, who applied all his medical knowledge, the child died only a short time later on 11 December 1897. The family were distraught. Having been elated at the news of his Magdalene's birth, Martin was devastated by the sad news of the baby's death. He had up to that point seemed to live a charmed life in Africa, not succumbing to the many hazards and diseases that most white people suffered, but the death of his daughter would have been a terrible blow to him. When Elvira returned they settled down to life together in Eldama Ravine. They were to have a second daughter three years later. She was born in Eldama Ravine Station and given the name of Eldoma. James Martin had founded a family at last, against the odds.

Soon after he resumed duty at Ravine, in August 1897, there were rumours of unrest among the Sudanese troops in Uganda. Contingents of men had been deployed by their superiors in expeditions to various parts of the country, resulting in long marches. For months the men had not seen their families and had been allowed little rest. The pay was miserable and the supply of clothing delayed. A couple of British officers, who did not know the askaris' language, were unpopular. When a large force of some 300 men started on another long expedition to Juba on the coast to delineate the border with Italian territory, they had hardly got beyond Ravine when the men refused to obey orders. They stopped, declined to proceed any further and returned to Ravine. There they were addressed by Jackson and MacDonald, but they refused to parley and started marching back on the long trek to Uganda, with the intention of joining up with other Sudanese askaris. They got as far as Lubas, where they were surrounded by MacDonald and loyal forces made up of Baganda and Swahili troops. Here at Lubas, where Bishop Hannington had been murdered, there were armed clashes and mutineers shot three British officers, while a fourth officer was killed in action. The mutinous askaris were, however, contained in their fortified enclosure, and pinned there for several months until one night they managed to sneak away. They were followed by loyal troops, and were finally beaten and dispersed. By February 1898 the mutiny was over. Meanwhile, back at Ravine, Martin was having a worrying time. There were still a small number of armed Sudanese troops under his charge at the station. With his excellent spoken Swahili and Arabic he had won their confidence and loyalty to the extent that he had persuaded the military commander to let them retain their arms – the only post in East Africa to be given this privilege while the mutiny lasted. Martin wisely took the precaution of increasing the number of armed Zanzibari porters in the camp.

In November 1897, in the midst of this tense situation, alarming reports were brought to Martin that a large force of over a thousand armed men with numerous camels was approaching Ravine from the direction of Abyssinia. He had not been told of the scientific expedition of Lord Delamere that had started at Berbera on the Red Sea and was proceeding through Somaliland and Abyssinia with the aim of reaching East Africa. He called his clerk de Silva and dictated a letter to be despatched immediately to the intruders as they reached Lake Baringo. It was not addressed to anyone in particular and read: 'Sir, Please take notice that you are now on British soil. Any act of aggression on your part will be sternly resisted!' The barely legible signature looked something like 'J. Martin', and when Delamere asked the locals who the officer in charge of the area might be, he was told 'Bwana Martini', which made him wonder why an Italian was trying to control entry of his party into British East Africa. In the event, the expedition turned out to be much smaller and in no way threatening, but arriving unannounced as it did at the height of the Sudanese army mutiny, it put fear into Martin that his small district headquarters might have to oppose a large Abyssinian force advancing in aid of the Sudanese rebels. He had in fact sent a hurried message to warn the senior officer at Fort Ternan that armed help might soon be needed, and had immediately set his own men and porters to dig a deep trench around the station and to reinforce the protective defensive boundary fence and palisade.

On arrival at Eldama Station, Delamere was welcomed by the 'wiry little man' who was Her Majesty's Collector, of the District of Baringo. He spent a couple of days there and was entertained in the warm and lavish manner for which Martin was gaining a reputation. Martin would have set out a lavish meal for Delamere, as was his custom. His wife would have recently been back from Zanzibar, and the two of them would have focused their attention on this guest and given him the best possible reception. It must have been an interesting meeting: Martin, now the old veteran with all his local know-how, and the British representative of the area, on one side; and Lord Delamere on the other side of the table, seventeen years old – less than half Martin's age – from another world altogether. Eton educated, Hugh Cholmondeley had recently assumed the title of 3rd Baron Delamere on the death of his father, who had been in the military. It had been expected that he would also go into the armed forces, but his father's death freed him of that obligation and after having secured his inheritance, a 7,000 acre estate and the family ancestral home in Cheshire, he went in quest of adventure. Martin was intrigued by Delamere's mode of transport, which included 200 dromedary camels. They discussed the pros and cons of camels, which were better adapted to the hotter northern area than to the colder highlands. Martin would have also given an account of happenings in Uganda in return for Delamere's news of the wider world.

This meeting must have stayed

long in Martin's memory. The last time he had sat in front of nobility was in Malta as a young lad. This time *he* did the inviting, *he* had the information and *he* was in charge of the area – an area many hundred times the size of his native Malta, with as many more inhabitants. He owned his own house and, yes, he also had his own horse. Thinking back to his boyhood dreams, they had all been achieved, and in fact surpassed, in a rather short time. Could life get any better? Could anything cross his path to ruin this great yet fragile status he had achieved?

It would also have been an important meeting for Delamere. Martin was the first white person he had encountered living in the East Africa that was to be his future. After his initial expedition Delamere was to return to Kenya almost yearly for hunting trips. On one safari he was charged by a lion and knocked down, and his Somali gun bearer, Abdulla Ashur, saved him from being mauled by throwing himself on the lion. This gave Delamere the time to recover his rifle and shoot the animal. He came out of the incident with a wounded leg, from which he would never fully recover – he afterwards always walked with a limp. It was his initiation into the local dangers and also into the legends of the land. 'He survived a lion charge' was something that carried weight. It also showed the loyalty displayed by his African staff, which was based on respect, a common trait where the Africans built up an awe and respect of the white man that wasn't always deserved.

Delamere then began slowly to focus his interest less on hunting and more on the land and its inhabitants. He became close to the local people and respected the Maasai in particular, being one of the few Europeans who learned their language. In 1903, six years after his first visit, he acquired his first farm of 100,000 acres to fulfil his ambitions of becoming a successful large-scale farmer. Though he brought many ideas from his own estate in Cheshire, he had to start from scratch and for many years lived in a native-type grass-roofed mud hut. His approach to farming was largely trial and error and he experimented with crops and livestock. The information he gathered became the know-how upon which the Kenyan agricultural industry was eventually built. He cross-bred English and New Zealand sheep, chickens and cattle to try to come up with species that would thrive. However, he had many failures that nearly drove him to bankruptcy, and only his determination and love of the country kept him going. He was the first person to start a maize farm, together with a flour mill, which eventually began to bring in a profit eleven years after he had started out as a farmer there.

As other white settler farmers arrived, Delamere quickly became their spokesperson and his views were adopted as the political, spiritual and social norms of many of the white settlers. In a letter in 1903 he wrote:

"there can be no room for doubt that it is the mission of Great Britain to work continually for the training and education of the African toward a higher education, intellectual, moral and economic level than that which they had reached when the crown assumed the responsibility for the administration of this territory."

This suggested his dedication to the well-being of the local Africans and his respect for them, which must at the time have been the politically correct statement as far as the motherland was concerned. However, in 1927, twenty-four years later, he wrote: *'The extension of the European civilisation was in itself a desirable thing.'* He went on to say: '*The British race was superior to the heterogeneous Africa. Races are only now emerging from centuries of relative barbarianism, so the opening of new areas by means of genuine colonisation was thus to the advantage of the world.*' Delamere was reflecting the thoughts of many of his fellow white settlers, showing how attitudes and aspirations had changed over the years. The white colony had become a law unto itself and felt that the government in Britain understood it less and less.

The aims and morals of some of the settlers had indeed certainly changed: the good life was having its effect. They liked the regime in Kenya, and there were even discussions about 'self-rule' apart from

Britain. Westminster's democratic wisdom seemed less relevant and had little reach in this faraway country. This tendency of the whites to want to 'keep' the land politically and not just agriculturally motivated the local people to form oppositions. It was those educated by the missionary schools rather than the government system that began to speak up. People like Jomo Kenyatta, the Luo Odinga Odinga and Tom Mboya started their quest to achieve a 'one man, one vote' political solution. It should, however, be noted that the majority of the Kenya white farmers were good hard-working people who were a credit to their homelands and did much good.

That first meeting with Martin in Kenya must have fired up Delamere's imagination. They may not have realised it, but it was a meeting of a first-generation Kenya settler/explorer with the next generation of settler/farmer. The baton was being handed on.

*****

When the Sudanese mutiny was over early in 1898, Martin returned to his normal duties as administrator. This, however gave him little power over the tribal social orders and rituals, some of which he approved of; others, such as the role of women and the female circumcision rites, were accepted as an evil of the package. He also acted as the 'Collector of Baringo District' – that is, he was responsible for collecting poll tax. He had the unenviable task of travelling on foot to tribal areas to collect payment from untamed inhabitants who had never been faced with a demand for the payment of any sort of tax before. When he first visited the wild Suk tribe for this purpose, he had wondered whether he would come out alive as he was rapidly surrounded by fierce chanting warriors. Once again the resourceful Martin extricated himself by a ruse. Seeing some good Somali ponies that belonged to the chief, he suggested that the chief should exchange some of these ponies for some of Martin's powerful *dawa* –

consisting of a couple of bottles of potent brandy, which the Chief was not averse to tasting during the bartering process. Martin himself was a teetotaller, but this did not prevent the bartering being protracted until well into the night. The next morning the chief, feeling quite miserable and heavy in the head, pleaded for some more 'medicine' until eventually he was ready to agree to anything, including allowing some of his best ponies to be led away by Martin in payment of the poll tax. Martin was shrewd. He had started trading on his own account, and there is little doubt that only part of the haul of ponies was needed to cover the tax.

While he was employed with the British East Africa Company, practically all his time had been spent on the march and he had not had much opportunity for private trading. Admittedly he did not entirely neglect the chance of purchasing goods at a cheap price at the coast and selling them en route to Buganda or disposing of them at a profit in Kampala itself. There was plenty of ivory to be had in the form of elephant tusks, and the profit margin on its sale at Mombasa was good. It would not have been beyond the resources of the leader of a caravan returning empty to the coast to utilise the porters for this trade. As a District Officer at Eldama Ravine, Martin was not supposed to engage in private trading, but there were no regulations stipulating this in the early days of the Uganda Administration. The first officers to be appointed were not formally recruited into the Service but were merely transferred en bloc from the IBEA Company. Through the staging post of Eldama passed all the private traders with their caravans. These were organised by Arabs striving to replace the profits of the slave trade by less questionable operations. There were also a few European adventurers who came to seek a fortune in East Africa, chief among them the red-headed Irishman Charles Stokes. He sold guns wherever he could and bought vast quantities of ivory with the proceeds. He combined his trading with the organisation of large caravans to escort missionaries and carry supplies. Initially a missionary, he had married one or more Africans who bore him children. He dressed up as an Arab trader, though his pale skin and his thick red beard showed that he hailed from a different part of the world. He was reckless, broke all the rules and became rich.

During the six years that he lived at Eldama Station, Martin also worked for some time for the construction of the new railway. The railway, later called the lunatic railway, was a story apart and perhaps one of the most eventful of Victorian construction projects, that has been recorded, filled with diversity.

16 Changing the natural order

It was about three in the morning. The night sky was clear but it was perhaps the light coming from a nearly full moon that made him uneasy. As he approached the outskirts of the village his instincts began telling him that all was not right. The goat on its own tied up outside just didn't fit. He preferred the cover of darkness. His instinct sounded alarm bells, so he began to edge cautiously back, keeping low, moving away from the situation he was in. Then he saw a flash and heard a loud crash and felt a heavy punch on his shoulder which knocked him to the ground. Dazed but still conscious, he struggled to stand up again and using all his considerable power he tried to start running, but there was another flash, this time above and ahead of him. He lost consciousness and then he lost his life. That was on 9 December 1898.

Only six months earlier, he had been sitting under a low-hanging thorn tree that gave him plenty of shade. He had chosen this vantage point in a crop of trees up on a hill with a clear vista of the flat Thika planes below. It was midday and hot, too hot to be out in the sun. His mood was black; he felt humiliated. He had just lost a fight and his wounds were still hurting. If he hadn't retreated, he would have suffered even more serious injury. It was not his game plan, but this was where he was now. The reality of the situation still teased his aggression. He was uncomfortable and disgruntled. This was his territory, and he should be the chief, but he was undergoing a major shift in his attitude. The vision he saw in front of him was not the image he saw in his mind. This worried him. Perhaps he was a bit disoriented. It was not a pretty picture. His instinct was to act on the incongruence of the situation. He had to act to get even, at least to set the score right in his own territory. Added to this, and in fact above all his life drivers, he was hungry.

So it was, insofar as lions can think in images, and accordingly make decisions and thus map their future actions. He was a rogue male lion and he and his colleague had just lost the fight to take over the pride, a male and seven lionesses, that occupied the neighbouring territory. The huge leader of the pride, with his fearsome black mane, had fought a vicious battle and had won decisively. The pride had been encircled him, and when he struck out with his paws and a loud roar at their leader, one of the females attacked him from behind and bit into the muscles of his thigh. It was a warning bite, not an all out 'to kill' bite. If he had turned to face off his attacker behind, he would have exposed his throat to the lion in front. He wasn't going to make that potentially fatal mistake. It was a hopeless situation. He couldn't cover both sides at once. If he fought on he would surely be killed; the odds were against him. So he turned and ran off, pursued by the other lions who instinctively chased anything running away. This was not the usual fight over sharing of prey, or getting some piece of another lion's kill. It was more fundamental. It was about controlling territory; it was about access to the females in the pride; it was about existence.

Lions are one of the most sociable of animal species, so in a fight among lions it is important to 'sway the crowd'. It is about winning the confidence of the females and opposing the male and seeing him off. So there is a strategic, social showmanship component to winning the fight, not just power alone. The dominant male uses the symbol of his mane to show power and authority over his pride. A large black mane is an accepted symbol and impresses the lionesses. It is a symbol that was borrowed by the British Empire, where the male lion with a large mane is a significant symbol of power. The symbol is also widely used in European heraldry. Kings, chiefs and presidents often dress up and accentuate their shoulders and throats in modified copies of the lion's mane. Kings have taken on names, such as Richard the Lionheart, to cash in on the lion's authority. The mane is every bit as powerful among the lionesses and is an important trait for sexual selection. The losing lion here was one of the Tsavo species that don't grow manes, so was thus at a disadvantage in trying to gain the support of the lionesses in order to win his fight.

He would, he hoped, one day, be back to fight the same battle again and get into that pride of lionesses. It was in his instinct. The fifty square miles of land which they 'ruled' usually had so much game but they had moved on, partly to get greener pastures and partly because they were pushed out. So another reason that he had to encroach into the pride's territory was so that he could get more opportunities for food. The pride hunted in the open savannah area where it was easier to stalk and kill prey. There were also more animals in that area – impala, wildebeest, Thomson's gazelle. The pride defended their territory viciously. This had pushed him out from this better plain land to the thicker scrublands. Here, low stunted 'wait-a-bit' thorn trees with thick undergrowth covered the land. Not only was there less game in this thicker bush, but it was more difficult to hunt because he could not get the length of space he needed to reach his top speed of 35 miles per hour to enable him to outrun his prey and catch them.

The drought recorded in 1897 in the Taita-Taveta area had played havoc with the environment and everything was affected: plants, insects, birds, wild game, elephants, even lions and of course humans. The Taita tribe were particularly hard hit. It was know as the Mwakisenge famine and led to an almost total ecological breakdown. Many of the Taita tribe of this area (also known as Tsavo) died; but worse, they fought, killed and even ate one another, and the many that died were not buried in the usual manner as there were so many of them. They were left outside in the open not far from their villages. Again, the disorder in the human world would impact the life of the lions.

The lion was at the top of this food chain, so as the mix and availability of his food changed he had to adapt, and he did. That's what lions do. That's why they are still king of the animal kingdom. The normal course of action of lions throughout history would be to change the animal prey they killed – maybe move from wildebeest to the smaller dik-dik to cover their need for 50 kilos of meat every two weeks. It might even be an option to kill elephants – a possible last resort that had been necessitated before. This was not without its dangers, and lions needed back-up: a full pride attacking in a group would be essential, otherwise the risk of getting gored by an elephant's tusk was too great. Being a sociable species and living in groups, lions learned in groups and also hunted in groups. Their power came from their closely knit understanding of one another's roles. But this lion did not have the strategic hunting power of a pride, so he did not decide to pursue any of the normal hunting/survival options. His mind was leading him towards another course of action that was taboo for Africa, beyond the natural order as God had intended.

There were two additional rational reasons 'forcing' him to break with the centuries-old traditions and habits of his kind – a break that would make him the most famous, or infamous, lion in history. The first of these reasons is not immediately apparent, but white men coming down from the Sudan had brought with them cattle infected with rinderpest. An epidemic had broken out which had slowly run south through East Africa around 1895. The local cattle had never before been exposed to this virus and died by the hundreds. The fallout caused by this epidemic was profound and especially affected the nomad Maasai tribe who lived mainly off their cattle. The previous year the epidemic had hit the Macharkos area to the north of the lion's territory.

The Africans used to cast out the dead cattle in the bush beside their villages, to be eaten by scavengers like hyenas and vultures. The dead carcasses were usually devoured and had disappeared by the next day, maintaining a healthy environment. However, due to the number of cattle that died at the same time from the epidemic, the carcasses thrown out were too many for the usual 'clean-up' scavengers. This provided an opportunity for the lion. Now, one of the lion's best-held secrets is that he does, from time to time, scavenge like 'vulgar' hyenas, wild dogs and vultures. (The noble lion was believed only to kill his own food and not feed off the scraps of other animals' prey, but this was not always so.) Thus during the rinderpest epidemic, dead cattle, which were easy to find, became the normal food for the lions of the area. This brought them closer to the villages than before, and their age-old fear of humans and of the African village that had built up began to dissipate. They became more used to the scent of humans and less perturbed by the noises they made. Noise was the one thing that normally scared lions, particularly the beating of tins and drums that was used by the villages to chase them away. But with this gradual acclimatisation, village outskirts began to be seen as potential areas for finding food.

Hence many more opportunities occurred for human–lion contact. In the present case, this was made worse by the fact that only a few days earlier the lion had found a human body left not far from the latest camp of railway workers who had just moved into the area – a most unusual occurrence. This gave the lion a taste of human meat for the first time. Almost gifted to him, it was a pleasant surprise. The second reason for his change in eating habits was that he suffered from a rotting broken tooth. The tooth had been broken in a wildebeest kill attempt, when he had got the animal by the back of the neck and the wildebeest's horn had twisted into his face and broken off his tooth. The tooth was painful, even more so when he ate tough meat like wildebeest. His experience of eating human flesh was a lot easier on the tooth as the soft tissue gave him less pain.

This combination of events, this ecological disaster – part of which was fate, part the result of the white man's intrusion into the area – made him resolve to go out that night and hunt for live prey from the camps. The action would be condemned, and he would be called a devil and a monster, and few would understand that he was only defending his right and his life. It would be over 150 years before people would understand his actions in a more positive light.[18] With his mind made up the lion, together with a hungry collaborator,stalked the nearby railway workers' camp. The decision was the difficult part; the actual hunt was far easier. The lion saw an open tent, crept in and grabbed the human by the throat. The human let out a short sharp cry, but was quickly silenced. The lion then dragged the body out of the camp and ate it about 500 yards away with colleague, who had stayed at a slight distance. It was done. They were 'the man-eating lions of Tsavo', to be known throughout the world, and to be hunted down and shot.

James Martin was at that time responsible for the recruitment of men for the construction of the railway. He had worked for Mr Whitehouse, the chief engineer, as a sort of manager and 'man of all trades' on and off since 1895. The man eaters must have been one of his biggest problems at the time. They roamed free for nine months after that first kill, until they were eventually shot. The whole affair was at first believed to be a rumour, but when the surviving eye-witnesses told their story, and this was backed up by traces of lion paw prints together with marks on the ground where the victims had been dragged away, and then finally the remains of the bodies were found, fear and panic began to grow. It culminated in a full-blown mutiny, with the work force fighting one another, and several men were murdered. The management needed all their skills to regain control of the situation. At one point work was halted for three whole weeks. Victims were taken one by one – a native, then an Indian, then the Irish engineer O'Hara, who was dragged off while sleeping next to his family. The lions even ripped through the tents to get at their victims. Sometimes the screams of the occupants were loud enough to frighten him away. Once a lion grabbed the mattress that a Greek contractor was sleeping on and carried it off. The man remained unhurt but was traumatised by the incident. Worst of all were the attacks on the hospital tents, when either patients or staff might be taken. No one was safe from this terror that surrounded the railway workers in the middle of the bush. Martin no doubt used his know-how to fortify the camps into *bomas*, with a thick ring of protective thorn trees around the outside. Even this, however, proved not to be wholly successful. In all, it was recorded that many natives, twenty-eight Indians and several Europeans were killed by lions.

If at the end of the world there is something like a reckoning or summary judgment of the species, the condemned 'man eaters of Tsavo' may yet get a reprieve. The lions, like Martin, were essentially part of the history of that great railway which was to open in 1899. Lt. Col. J. H. Patterson, an engineer, was responsible for the construction of the railway at the time, having taken over from a Mr O. Preston after the railway reached Voi, halfway to Nairobi. Patterson, an expert at bridge-building, took it upon himself to hunt the lions down. The loss of personnel to the lions was obviously a major problem, and the nine months' delay in capturing the lions a serious failure on the part of the management. Whether this lion was not properly targeted, or whether Patterson, although insisting on shooting it himself, was not really qualified to do so, a rather a messed up job.

Martin's expertise was initially the recruitment of local tribes as construction workers for the railway. His forte was making things work at the local level, but here he was not able to get enough people with the skills and willingness to do the labouring work. The chief engineer, Mr Whitehouse, had a mass of contacts for willing and cheap labour from his recent experience building the Indian railways, so it was decided to import workers from India. Initially 2,600 workers were brought in from the sub-continent, increasing to a total of over 30,000. This was in addition to the hundreds of local labourers used on the project. The loss of labour to lions, although dramatic, was only a fraction of the total loss of life during the construction of the 587-mile railway. Records show that of the 31,983 Indians contracted to do the work, 2,493 (8%) died and a further 6,000 suffered accidents and became invalids. That is, 26% of the workforce were affected during the five-year construction. Each of these individuals had his own horror story. A total of 6,794 (about 21%) stayed behind in East Africa and formed the future Asian community which was to bring much prosperity to the country. The railway was a feat of engineering and a great achievement, but at a cost that is difficult to understand from our viewpoint today. Life was indeed vicious for all involved – the locals, the Indians, the whites and even the lions.

During this time Martin would have worked on the numbering system he had developed to compensate for his dyslexic shortcomings. It must have been in full use in order for him to keep up with numbers of employees engaged. He apparently had a complex system of 'hieroglyphics' that only he understood, but the bookkeeping functioned well. It would be interesting to know how he solved his problem – in effect inventing a new numbering system. To compensate for the deficiencies in the link-ups in his dyslexic brain, he must have created new pathways to replace the ones he couldn't use. The important thing was that he was able to function in the real world, albeit with a patched-up, pieced together and improvised mental system, which worked, but was no match to the fully educated, orthodox model.

The railway work added substantially both to Martin's reputation and to his salary. On getting back to his Ravine base he increased his income still further by trading and used his position to enable himself and his family to live in lavish style. He spent a good deal on entertaining guests and showering them with hospitality, and must have become the envy of less enterprising officers. His trading activities eventually attracted the attention of his superiors, and would have drawn serious censure on him had he not already been something of a legend in East Africa, and had he not had many friends and protectors, among them Sir Frederick Jackson. However, at a convenient moment Martin was eased out of his lucrative posting and sent to one of the islands in Lake Victoria with the task of building an official station there. This was a kick in the teeth.

17 Rollercoaster ride (1904–1914)

After leaving Ravine, Martin remained in the Lake Victoria's Ssese Islands for only a brief period. He did not fancy the crocodiles or the hippopotami that abounded near the island shores, and he intensely disliked the mosquitoes and flies that intruded everywhere. In particular he was nauseated by the periodical appearance of the all-pervading lake flies. These flies bred in their millions in the waters of the lake, and rose like minute bubbles to burst on the surface and release an immense cloud of flying insects that filled and darkened the sky for miles around. They were impossible to avoid. The flies that were blown ashore by the breeze dropped down to earth and, dying, emitted a repulsive fishy smell that pervaded the atmosphere and hung around for days. The horrors of the 'Mosquito Coast' were as nothing compared to this. The Ssese Islands were a dead end. They were not on any trading route and were only accessible by boat – and this in the middle of country that was itself, virtually inaccessible. Even the local Africans didn't want to live there and the islands were very sparsely populated. Even today the Ssese Islands are still a backwater. It seemed to him like a jail sentence rather than a posting, and the normally free-living Martin came to understand the power, arbitrariness and malice that his superiors' decisions could sometimes have.

By then suitably humbled, he was glad when he was rehabilitated and posted to Entebbe as District Officer and Collector. Entebbe, on the north of the Great Lake, was, on the other hand, a rapidly growing centre of the British protecting power and had become the gateway to Uganda. Travellers arrived by the newly completed railway that steamed its way from Mombasa on the coast to its terminal point at Port Florence on Lake Victoria; thence they crossed by lake steamer to Port Alice at Entebbe. The long, laborious hauling of goods and supplies for Uganda on the heads of Zanzibar porters had all but died out; the railway replaced it seemingly overnight, bringing commerce and progress and contact with the outside world all along the safari route. For Martin, Entebbe was a mixed blessing. He had plenty to do as a District Officer dealing with people's problems in and around Entebbe. He knew the local Baganda people and their Luganda language from some of his earlier trips, so much was familiar to him. He had arrived at a time when the future township was being laid out with roads and parks and new buildings – mainly offices and dwellings for government officials and for Indian and Goan workmen. The laying-out of the Botanical Gardens on the lake shore, for instance, involved the engagement of over a thousand labourers. His official duties included meeting important visitors on their arrival and attending their departure at Port Alice pier.

Among these dignitaries were the Duke of Abruzzi who, with a party of Italian Alpine troops, had come on a mountain-climbing expedition to the Ruwenzoris – the fabled Mountains of the Moon. Martin, whose Italian came into full play again, accompanied him from Entebbe with an escort of twenty-six askaris and sixty-seven porters, and travelled with him, flying the British and Italian flags, to the foothills of the impressive mountain range. As a keepsake Martin was presented with one of two hunting rifles bearing the Duke's arms that had been specially made for the Duke by Greener. (The gun is still in the possession of Martin's family.) Another visitor of repute whom Martin met at Entebbe was Winston Churchill. As Parliamentary Under-Secretary for the Colonies, Churchill arrived on 19 November 1907, clad in a white uniform and displaying an impressive row of medals. He was received by a guard of honour of Sudanese troops and was introduced to senior officers of the Protectorate. There were no cars in Uganda in 1907 and Churchill travelled to Kampala by rickshaw – a distance of twenty-six miles, which was accomplished in three hours. The officers who accompanied him went on bicycles. After a short visit, Churchill left Uganda via Sudan.

The missionary order of the White Fathers found Martin very helpful.

Their headquarters were at Rubaga, in Kampala, but they had set up a mission school and hospital at Kisubi, a couple of miles outside Entebbe. They now wished to build a church adjoining the house at Entebbe, and Martin assisted them in choosing a suitable site at Bugonga, an area of about two acres for which £25 was paid. He made them a gift of the timber needed for constructing the benches. Later he presented the church with one of the three bells that now hang in the belfry. While the church was under construction Martin's house was used for religious worship, and he accommodated the father in charge until the church was ready. He proposed that the mission should build a nuns' convent for the care and education of young Africans. He also selected the site for the Entebbe cemetery, which he then divided into four sections: one each for the Catholics, the Protestants, the Moslems and the pagans. Martin saw a good deal of the White Fathers at Entebbe, and he is frequently mentioned in the daily diary that they were obliged by the rules of their Order to maintain. There is a reference in the Mission diary to an inquiry conducted by

Martin, on 20 July 1905, into the case of the sale of a girl from Kisubi by her uncle for thirty rupees. Her father had agreed to the deal, taking most of the money for himself. The girl was being forced to turn Moslem; she refused, escaped and sought refuge with the White Fathers. Around this time several young Baganda were sent by the Entebbe White Fathers to the island of Malta to be educated and trained as doctors. On their return, many of them made quite a name for themselves in government service during an epidemic of smallpox. Meeting them would have been the first contact Martin had in Africa with people who had lived in his own country.

When James Martin finally left Entebbe, the White Fathers said he was a 'good and generous friend'. He saw the positive effects the missionaries were having on teaching the local population and was more then happy to contribute to their work, although he does not appear to have been an unduly good practising Catholic himself. When, on the occasion of the marriage of his daughter to a Mr Tarrant at Entebbe, he attended Holy Mass, the

Mission diary records that 'he departed from his usual habit in order to accompany Mr Tarrant at Mass'. Having said that, one must mention that his manner of life at sea and later on constant safari was hardly conducive to the practice of religion. However, after he was married in Zanzibar in civil form before the British Consul, he later took pains to have his marriage blessed by a Catholic priest at Eldama Ravine Station, and he arranged for his daughter, Eldoma, to be christened.

Martin was now fifty years old. He was still very active and ready to put his hand to anything, but as the work of administering the country developed and became more technical and more decentralised, the verbal thinking skills that he hardly possessed were more and more in demand. His position was becoming increasingly difficult to maintain.

18 Losing the battle

James Martin's usefulness lay in his ability to speak several African languages, with Swahili and Luganda in the lead, as well as in his resourcefulness and his uncanny perception of what would impress the native mind. His popularity in Entebbe was unrivalled, while his long and vast experience of East Africa gave him a clear advantage over many other District Officers in the field. However, he came down badly in the matter of written instructions, reports or correspondence, as he was helpless without the aid of a trusted clerk or friend. The problems that arose because of his illiteracy had never been light and they now increased to the extent that he frequently became more of a burden than a help. The ingenious manner in which he covered up his lack of education caused much amusement. He avoided embarrassing situations by craftily skirting round a subject, or by breaking into one of his entertaining anecdotes – he was a past master in the art of recounting stories, whether genuine, fantastic or made up on the spur of the moment. His friends saw through this subterfuge, but Martin was so likeable that they accepted him as he was and made the necessary allowance for his weaknesses.

He was renowned for his hospitality, and this no doubt helped. At the Entebbe club bar he was wont to offer rounds of drinks and to good-humouredly tell his friends: 'You sign – I pay!' On occasions he was known to avoid writing or signing his name by claiming that he did not have his spectacles with him – though none of the photographs of him ever showed him wearing spectacles. He is said to have repeatedly used this ruse when dealing with court cases as a junior magistrate. It seems impossible that anyone should have been allowed to conduct a trial with this degree of illiteracy, but his uncanny understanding of the Africans' mentality, of their customs and reactions to situations, made him a fair judge, even if not all of the technicalities of the law were always followed. Of course, he had to lean heavily on his clerk, and when the time came to read the sentence he invariably ask the clerk to read it.

Another consideration that brought pressure on Martin's job was that once the British government had formed the East African Protectorate (having taken it over from the IBEA), they proceeded to introduce a more structured and formal government organisation; the number of commissioners was thus increased. Originally there were fourteen (including Martin) but in 1904 this had increased to 240. The commissioners consisted of the old IBEA Company employees, new recruits from other African countries and new recruits from England. In their quest for higher standards in the Secretariat and no doubt with the wish to 'move on' some of the older, more experienced administrators and replace them with freshly trained people, they relied on bureaucracy. Martin was therefore subjected to a lot more competition, particularly for the good jobs. One of their selection measures gave an indication of how they operated. Around 1907 the Secretariat brought in a new policy, and all Secretariat officers had to undergo the following test: all the words of the following sentence had to be spelt correctly:

It is agreeable to perceive the unparalleled embarrassment of the harassed peddler while gauging the symmetry of a peeled potato before a committee of judgement.[18]

This was a requirement for an administrator of the African territories. It seemed like a scheme concocted by the 'New Guard of Administrators' to clear out some of the older, less literate but more practical men.

The new men were clearly university-trained 'verbal thinkers' and derived their information from books, without paying too much attention to stories or images of the past. Whether or not the illiterate Martin was asked to take this test is unknown. With all his experience and knowledge of the native languages, and all he had done to help the locals and to support traders in difficult situations, he must have felt the weight of injustice fall upon him. He was under tremendous pressure to maintain and improve his status, which was part of his identity and which he had been so successful at developing. He used every trick of his active mind to defend his position. However, the many and increasing tests that he was subjected too by his younger colleagues – some seemingly posed to ridicule him – clearly showed others and then himself that he was not 'up to the mark'. The blocks that existed in his mind could not be successfully circumvented any more. Innate wisdom told him it was no longer his environment: the writing was on the wall.

A move would, all in all, be a welcome change for Martin, who had now been in the Secretariat for thirteen years. While it had given him a good position and great opportunities, he was not always at ease with the direction in which the Secretariat was going. Martin's own tendency to work with the locals and assist them with education, family and health would have been in conflict with the more 'military' stance of the Administration. He worked at the 'sharp edge' and had to make decrees palatable and acceptable to the natives. This sense of conflict was shared by many of the missionaries too. The definitive statement of the Administration's views, made by Sir Charles Eliot, the High Commissioner, in 1900, was perhaps a negative turning point. He said that it was only a few years since the place had been a human hunting ground, where the native tribes warred with each other to get slaves to sell to Arabs, and therefore:

"We are not destroying any old or interesting system, but simply introducing order into blank, uninteresting, brutal barbarism ... East Africa is not an ordinary Colony. It is practically an estate belonging to His Majesty's Government, on which an enormous outlay has been made and which ought to repay that outlay."[19]

What Eliot suggested as a means to achieve this was an influx of white settlers to develop the country and utilise the railway. This would transform the whole protectorate. But Martin probably couldn't help thinking that this was not the way the British had administered Malta, where there was no outsider land-grabbing, and wondering whether it was the right way. He knew that the Africans valued their land, although it was clearly under-utilised, and taking it over, perhaps by dubious means, would have repercussions. This policy would clash with the fundamental motivation of the natives to 'own their piece of land'. Even areas that were uncultivated were still part of their land in their own eyes, and they had fought for it over generations. The Maasai, for instance, as semi-nomads, claimed the vast territories that they moved within to be theirs. There would probably be more conflict ahead.

Another thing that no doubt made Martin feel uncomfortable was the rigid hierarchical system that the Secretariat had brought in. When he began, there had been nineteen officers. The attrition rate was high: of the twenty people in post in 1887, seven had died by 1907 and the death rate of the newcomers was much the same. Mainly they died of disease – often blackwater fever, a malaria-like illness. Most of these people had arrived with no knowledge of the country. They were divided into higher officers and lower officers, and each group had its own social club. They tended to see the rest of the new society they were forming as a hierarchy consisting of the whites, the white settlers, the new influx of Indians and the native Africans. Each of these groups had its own elaborate sub-hierarchy, particularly the Indians. The complexity of the African tribal system with its sixty or so tribes was made even more complicated with the addition of these hierarchies – an intricate order to manage. On top of all this were the many religions represented, which cut across racial divides.

As Martin's wife was a darker-coloured Portuguese she was sometimes taken to be Indian or Goan, which had led to one or two awkward racial situations: people sometimes assumed Martin to be in one social strata and his wife in another. Although frowned upon by the Administration, a few bachelor officers in remote areas had native mistresses, or even concubines, and gave no status to their partners. This was again 'socially incongruent'. The resulting children, of mixed race were ignored by the white community, but they luckily found easy acceptance in the more tolerant African circles. The administrative climate exacerbated the racial divide rather than minimising it, and it was a strange, changing and complex phenomenon. In any newly forming society, the initial vision or structure tends to perpetuate until an eventual crisis readjusts the social gulfs it has created. In this case the structures became more entrenched, and more and more levels formed as time went on, rather than there being a movement towards a single, more integrated melting pot. The new white administrators at the top spent less and less time talking to the grassroots African tribesmen in the way Martin had done.

Early in 1907, an opportunity arose for Martin to be eased out of his job in government service without embarrassment. The manager of the large Mabira Forest Rubber Company was leaving Uganda on his retirement, and Martin was offered the manager's job at a higher remuneration than his own government salary. The solution undoubtedly accommodated Martin. He could live in comfort while controlling a large body of African labourers, something that was well within his competence. He could keep up his friendships in nearby Kampala and Entebbe, and his new home at once became known for its hospitality. When he visited his friends he went laden with gifts, and returned with presents that had been pressed upon him. But he did not know the value of money and made no provision for his old age.

19 The lost war that was won (1914–1918)

Martin's leisurely life at Mabira came to an end with the start of the Great War in 1914. Even at the age of sixty he insisted on doing his bit for the Empire by seeking a commission in the Intelligence Corps and going to the front at Kagera river, on the western shores of Lake Victoria, which marked the dividing line between the opposing German and British forces. The story is told of how Lieutenant J. Martin was pulled along the front line in a rickshaw, wearing carpet slippers! He was very much a part of the bravado and war spirit that caught the colony: 'we must do our bit for the country' and 'show we are British'. The joyous expectation of marching off to war and all boarding the banner-waving trains to the sound of military brass bands was intoxicating. No doubt old friends were brought together again and many an old tale told. Their wives and families were left behind in the cities or on the farms or returned to their home countries in Europe. The belief that they were the best and knew this land inside out pushed them on to test their 'manliness'.

There was, however, no need for this local war, and initially the parties had agreed to stick with an 1886 agreement which stated that the colonies would remain neutral in the face of conflicts in Europe. It need not have affected life in the colonies. In spite of this, it was the British who struck first, on the shores of Lake Victoria – ownership of the lake, which both Germans and British shared, being the target – and from then on things predictably escalated.

The first big campaign was the two-pronged attack that the British planned, one prong being an amphibious assault with 8,000 troops on Tanga near the coast. This would control the gateway to the sea and the eastern railway terminus. The second was inland, with 4,000 troops in the Kilimanjaro area to take the western railway terminus. The plan was that both would break through and meet in the middle. Although outnumbered 8:1 in Tanga and 4:1 in Kilimanjaro, the Germans prevailed on both fronts. The Battle of

Tanga and the Battle of Kilimanjaro were among the most notable failures in British Military History.

A large part of the blame was levelled at the intelligence that was used to plan the battle – information provided by the corps that Martin was working for. It was reported that the Germans had 200 men in the Kilimanjaro area; in fact they had 600 askaris and 86 sharp young well-trained Germans on horseback. It would perhaps not be fair to attribute this misunderstanding to Martin's limited ability in reading numbers. The British East Africa forces suffered heavy losses of life and materials. The make-up of their numbers had consisted of many white Kenya settlers and farmers, who prided themselves as good shots with a rifle and had a belief in their superiority, but they were not properly trained in sharp military tactics. Many a Kenya volunteer farmer returned to home licking his wounds; many others never got back at all.

One fascinating anecdote is recorded about Martin's war service. The

German light cruiser and armed raider *Koenigsberg* had been roaming the South Atlantic and the Indian Ocean, sinking Allied shipping and spreading terror wherever she went. She even closed on Zanzibar Harbour when the British cruiser HMS *Pegasus* was having her boilers cleaned and was thus immobilised. The *Koenigsberg* sank HMS *Pegasus* at her moorings and then withdrew to German East Africa to escape the Allied warships that were now pursuing her. She entered the winding Rufiji river and withdrew up it as far as she could, and there felt herself safe from naval attack, for the water was shallow and the refuge hidden from view. The *Koenigsberg*, however, could not escape her final destiny. The Royal Navy sent out from Malta (by coincidence) two special ships with a shallow draught, one a monitor armed with a sixteen-inch gun. The monitor could navigate up the Rufiji close enough to hit the German raider. This she did, led on her way by a small tug piloted by James Martin. After this incident the British fared better, but never really won the war in East Africa as it turned into a stalemate. In the end the Germans had to surrender along with the general armistice. This brought an end to the German influence in that region and the Tanzania region reverted to Great Britain.

The final count of the war in East Africa was 10,000 British Commonwealth forces lost to war or disease. It was recorded that the Germans only lost 2,000 dead – a tactical victory. The true losers were the black soldiers and population who lost near on 100,000 from both sides. Black civilians also suffered in high numbers. This unnecessary war devastated many localities, bringing hunger, disease and death in its wake. The cosy colonial order built up over the previous seventy years, which had begun to develop some coexistence, was now in ashes. The white order, which had seemed so infallible to many Africans, proved to be as fragile as their own previous existence. The whole affair must have ripped up much of the trust built over the years between locals and settlers. The awe of the 'white system' had been severely dented, and much of the good work that Martin and others had done had been lost because of the devastations of the

20 The good, the bad and the ugly

After the war it seemed that the world had changed – the second big change that Martin had seen (the first had been when the railway arrived in Nairobi). The war was won, but it seemed that the economy and the people were the losers. The company he worked for had suffered with their rubber exports during the war and there was no work for him there now. The whole of East Africa, like many places in Europe, was in a depression, with little or no work anywhere. But if it was bad in Europe, it was worse in East Africa. Martin was seen in Mombasa in poor circumstances, like a bird fished out of the water, dejected and sad. The once part-time ivory trader was buying and selling chillies to keep himself afloat: his luck and his money had run out. The environment was harsh and he clearly could not cope in a new age that was so different from and so much more demanding than the one he had been used to. The dream had come to an abrupt end. His family probably convinced him to return to Portugal where some of Elvira's relatives lived, and having got together the money for their passage Martin and his family caught a ship bound for Lisbon.

Martin would have had time to stand at the stern of the ship and watch the churned sea wake created by the propellers, and look back at the outline of Africa as it receded into the distance until Mombasa was just a smudge on the distance horizon. He must surely have pondered on what his thirty-six years there had all meant and perhaps tried to put the things he had seen and the people he had met and known into an honest critical perspective.

He maybe wondered how others of his countrymen, the many who left home like himself, had fared in the outside world. Had they had similar adventures? Had they had more opportunities? Did they regret leaving? He certainly hadn't.

When he first arrived in Africa, sail had been faster than steam and moving a ship had involved setting the sails with every shift of wind and being totally dependent on the weather. Now there wasn't a sail in sight, and running a ship was no effort at all. Ships now went faster, and in a straight line. Not having to use the unpredictable power of the wind, sailors were in much less danger of being shipwrecked. The change in travelling around inside East Africa was even more amazing: a three-month journey on foot to Uganda, with all its hardships and hazards, had been replaced by an easy few days sitting down in a train compartment.

It was, however, the lives of the people that had changed the most. When he had arrived in Zanzibar the signs of slavery were everywhere. It was by far the worst thing that was happening. It was a human tragedy for each one of the slaves captured and meant death for many of them. He had come to realise also the consequences it had for the lives and minds of the people who were not themselves taken as slaves. They lived in fear of the 'spirit men', and this dread and superstition was used to control their way of life. Martin understood this effect from his childhood days, although not in the same measure, but he had outgrown it and knew the importance of conquering false notions and their power. It was also the cause of much inter-tribal conflict and it bred suspicion and mistrust. It was a poison that had become ingrained in their cultures. Slavery was a medium by which tribes or their chiefs could trade with the outside world and get essential products for their advancement, such as wire and beads for their work and personal decoration; food and grain in times of famine so that they could survive; and guns and weapons so that they could kill game to eat and also protect themselves against their enemy neighbours. It was difficult to quantify the massive change that removing slavery had brought. The creation of other forms of trade to enable the locals to buy what they needed without having to traffic slaves was an important factor in the change in which Martin had played a part. Developing honest trading bit by bit, the people slowly became more open to outsiders and trusted each other more. They began to work together; although tribal differences were always there, they became more manageable.

Martin had come to understand the natives' needs and problems, and that the vicious circle created by slavery had to be actively broken in order for progress to take effect. Knowing the cause of their anxieties and animosities often helped him to solve disputes and negotiate peaceful solutions, whether for the passage of one of his caravans or in the administration of his station at Eldama Ravine. He was gratified that he had potentially saved so many lives by being part of the group involved in ending the slave trade. It had been the cause of so much of the trouble and killing he had come across. Regarding relations between the tribes, one thing that was clear was that whereas before each tribe was isolated and did not have much contact with others, now the Luo talked with the Kikuyu and the Luhya with the Nandi, and so on. There was much more contact between the tribes, and not only in the melting pot of Nairobi.

The Europeans had initially

considered the indigenous people to be 'wild savages', but now the richness of their cultures and languages was known to many. The diversity and complexity of the different tribes that made up East Africa was a truly remarkable thing that no one had imagined at the beginning. He had certainly done his bit to proclaim the diversity of those societies. The fact that Martin couldn't read or write was seen as a disadvantage by his white colleagues and it had held him back and caused him much frustration, but he found that the Africans acquired information in the manner that he did and that his own way was better for communicating with them. So he stubbornly held on to his way of doing things; he believed that he had, in many ways, been ahead of his colleagues in communicating with the people because he had had to find a way to do it and he enjoyed it. He had been grateful to his clerk de Silva, who had helped him by doing his reading and writing. His illiteracy had kept him vulnerable, particularly in European social circles. He counteracted this with generosity, humour, know-how and a sharp memory, thus maintaining the respect of his friends and colleagues. Consequently, his humility had kept his feet on the ground. He must have regretted that his mass of knowledge about African people would not be written down and so would be lost.

Martin had, in the main, been altruistic in his approach to Africans. In terms of education and medical support and the prevention of disease, he had assisted the local people as far as he could, but this was not always easy. The circumstances had sometimes demanded hard reactions. Some of the chiefs were autocratic and irrational in their behaviour and in judging their fellow men; the Kabaka (chief) of the Buganda in Uganda was an example. Martin felt that he should prevent this and condemn it at any local tribe democratic councils or judgments when he was acting as District Commissioner.

There was an image in his mind of the way he remembered the British to have acted towards his own people at home in Malta. They had seemed to be there to help the Maltese, to bring them trade and business and protect them from other powers. They honoured the existing institutions of the people. There was no violence and no abuse of the Maltese, and no grabbing of land by incoming settlers. Yes, there had been the upper classes and the lower classes that clashed now and then, but the English had lived among them and associated with the upper-class Maltese on an equal basis, it seemed to him. He understood that there was less of a gulf between the British and the Maltese, with them both being European, than there was between the British and the African tribes, but he wondered why the approach that worked in Malta couldn't have been tried in Africa too. It could have all turned out so differently. He didn't often speak about this but it was what he felt.

The later white 'grab' of African land, no matter how much it was cloaked in contractual jargon, was not the best way. Disputes over property were always a problem. After the railways were built, many more white settlers were encouraged to move in and they bought up the natives' land, usually to much local protest. The settler farmers, like Delamere, who came from either South Africa or Britain were a varied group of people. Some built good farms and employed and taught farming to native staff – they were fine, hard-working people who did a great job of clearing wild land for cultivation. They taught the local people that farming wasn't just about providing for yourself but was about working together to produce a surplus for others and for the country as a whole. There were others, however, who abused the blacks at any opportunity. The circumstances in which they were given or bought their land were dubious, and often local chiefs were cheated into selling land without knowing it. Things became a lot clearer years later. Martin was glad he had never owned land; it had often been offered to him, but he wasn't a farmer and he instinctively felt that owning land was not the right thing to do.

There were also civil servants fresh out of Britain with their university degrees. They were willing and sincere but lacked knowledge of the local situation and very often tried to push views that were not always well received. Another category of people that Martin had met and didn't care for were the white ivory hunters. Their sole purpose was to kill as many of the magnificent elephants as possible: over 150 animals could be killed in a single trip. These people did have certain good points, however, and sometimes helped villages clear off elephants that were eating their crops. Once an elephant had been killed the vultures would circle above it, and this was the sign for the women of the village to go and hack meat from the dead animal, with the vultures pointing the way. The women would clamber into the carcass to get at the prized fat. An elephant kill was good meat and a celebration for the village, but the hunters' main purpose was greed and not any betterment of the locals. Some of the hunters, like 'Karamoja' Walter Bell, had become very rich and established large estates back in their home countries (in Bell's case, Scotland), leaving little behind in Africa. This wild hunting continued but became more moderate, and the hunters' exploitation of slavery stopped. The ivory trade, however, played its part in developing business in Africa and Martin had himself dabbled in the 'white gold'.

The many missionaries that he had got to know did a good job, and that achievement should not be underestimated. Many people now had a better education than he had had as a boy, which was good progress. Some of those missionaries pushed religion too hard, and this seemed to him out of place in the tribal cultures. However, some of the tribal traditions were not good and the missionaries had helped to get rid of them: for example, the influence of the witch doctors generally had a negative effect and could be criminal. The preachers were inclined to lord it over the natives without giving them a chance to develop their own culture. Some that he had met didn't cope well with the conditions and either went mad or became ill when they simply couldn't take it any more. They paid an awful price for having wanted 'to come and help the natives'.

He admired his friends and colleagues at the IBEA and in the British colonial government, but again some of them had a Victorian 'British Empire' approach and often a military background that made them authoritarian and sometimes ruthless. They often took the military option – too readily at times – as Frank Hall had done at Fort Smith: he had learned to deal forcibly with African dissent and then used the fear engendered to generate trust. (This was a typical blueprint for many of the colonisers.) Once when three of his mail men were murdered he undertook raids with 150 men and burnt and destroyed everything the rebels had. This was gross overreaction, and had given communication and negotiation little chance. Nevertheless, Frank went on to do much good work on road-building and became well respected by all, including the Kikuyu. Martin probably realised that in many ways he had done things differently, and that it was his far from perfect upbringing in Malta and his luck that had helped him survive as an exception.

There were other sad stories concerning some of the more aggressive natives – such as the Wakwafi tribe (a part of the Maasai) and their warriors – who after much conflict with caravans were eventually subdued by a series of disasters: the viral disease rinderpest came from the north (the Red Sea) and killed their cattle, and in 1889 smallpox and famine depleted their numbers. Internal conflict, disease, poverty and hunger further reduced the tribe. These were some of the regrettable aspects of what Martin had been a part of. It could all have been done better.

Although he couldn't read or write, when he looked at a map of Kenya he could see his old camp, now marked Nairobi, and a bump in the straight boarder with Tanzania, where his Taveta camp was. Fancy that! Nairobi was a refuge for people of all the different tribes who needed to escape situations in their local villages. It offered hope, and a way of mixing tribal living and modern opportunities. He must have also recalled all his African friends and the chiefs and remembered the good times they had had. His African friends did not forget him and seem to have paid him the ultimate compliment of naming their children after him. There is evidence of at least one Kenyan from the Kisumu/Luo region, born in 1975, who bears the name of James Martin.[20]

*****

Much of the story of Martin's times concerns the beginning of things, including the development of tolerance between cultures. Several journeys of social change cross paths in this biography. The first is the journey of progress of the black Kenyan, as exemplified in Barack Obama and described above: it covers the 120 years from Thomson and Martin's first meeting with the Luo tribe to Obama's US presidential nomination. It was the result of a benevolent approach towards the natives. Another – not the least – is the 'social journey' of the people of East Africa and their leaders today. Thanks must go to the many non-black missionaries, doctors, administrators, teachers, farmers, engineers and tradesmen who have, like Martin and since Martin's time, made East Africa their home. This social journey of understanding and acceptance is not yet completed, and nor is the role and dignity of the African women equitably established.

The East Africa that Martin loved had so many surprises: the good – among them the original birth place of human kind, not far from where Martin walked, the emergence of so many good people, like Obama, the great wealth and cities; the bad – which included the many conflicts to independence; and the ugly – which sowed seeds that led to the Great War and later to the Holocaust. Those early formative times were the beginning of so many things that impacted our integrated and linked world of today. They made the world smaller.

Very little else is known
about the life of our remarkable hero.
No doubt in the few remaining years
of his life he made new friends and
kept them entranced with his stories.
James Martin, alias Antonio Martini,
died in 1925 and was buried in Lisbon.
He was sixty-seven years of age.

****

Appendix 1: Tribes and languages of East Africa

Uganda Tribes

Bantu-speaking tribes

Central Region: Baganda

Western Region: Batooro, Banyoro, Bakiga, Bafumbira, Bakonjo, Bamba, Banyarwanda and Batwa

Eastern Region: Basoga, Banyuli, Bakenye, Bagishu, Bagwe,

North-Eastern Region: Bateso, Jopadhola and Karimojong, Kumam, Jonam, Sebi, Pokot (Suk) and Tepeth

Nilotic-speaking tribes

North Region: Acholi, Alur, Langi, Lugbara, Madi, Kakwa

North-Western Region: Lendus (also in Zaire)

Kenya Tribes

The hunter-gatherers

Boni, Dahalo, El-Molo, Ndorobo and Sanye

Bantu-speaking tribes (agriculturists)

Western Region: Luhya, Kisii, Kuria, Gusii

Central Region: Kikuyu, Kamba, Meru, Embu, Tharaka, Mbere

Coastal Region: The Mijikenda (Digo, Duruma,Rabai, Ribe, Kamba, Jibana, Chonyi, Giriama and Kauma);
Segeju, Taveta, Pokomo and Taita

Nilotes and Paranilotes (pastoralists)

***Nilote*:** Luo

Teso: Iteso, Turkana

Maasai: Maasai, Samburu, Njemps, Chagga

Kalenjin: Nandi, Kipsigis, Elgeyo, Sabaot, Marakwet, Tugen, Terik, Pokot

Cushites (shepherds)

Somali, Rendille, Galla, Borana, Gabra, Orma, Sakuye

Swahili (fishermen)

Bajun, Pate, Mvita, Vimba, Ozi,
Fundi, Siyu, Shela,
Amu

(Adapted from Nicholls, *Red Strangers*)

Appendix 2: Journeys on foot in East Africa performed by James Martin

1883: February 1883 to May 1884: sixteen-month safari with Joseph Thomson'through Masai Land'.

1885: 16 June: Journey to Chagga country with General Mathews.

11 September to 5 November: safari up Tana river with Sir R.G.Harvey.

1886 : With General Mathews on military expedition to Chagga Country.

December to May 1887: leader of big game hunting safari of Captain John Willoughby to borders of Maasailand.

1888: February to November: leader of safari of Sir Robert Harvey

1889: 18 June 1889 to 14 April 1890: l leader of caravan with Fredrick Jackson from Mombasa to Uganda.

1890: 14 May to 4 September: return to Mombasa in caravan with Jackson .

1891: 7 April too August: return safari to Mombasa. September to 9 December: safari caravan to Uganda .

1892: 8 January to 11 may: return safari to the coast.
August to 6 December: caravan leaves Mombasa for Uganda.
1893: January to May: return journey to Mombasa with large cargo of ivory.
31 Jul to October: fresh caravan for Uganda leaves Mombasa with Captain Eric Smith.
1894: Return journey to coast.
8 September: Uganda bound with W. Hobley, Foaker and Macallister. Martin joins Uganda Government Administration and goes to his new post at Eldama Revine.
1895: Martin Goes to Mombasa and then to Zanzibar to get married.
1896: Martin returns to Eldama Revine.

The above is not a comprehensive list, but every safari mentioned has been recorded in one or more books dealing with the early days in East Africa. The Royal Geographical Society stated that Martin had made no fewer than twentythree trips travelling from Mombasa to Uganda or back. The distance from Kampala to the coast was estimated to be 800 miles.

Appendix 3: Martin's age

Listing in the Uganda Pension List in *Uganda Blue Book*, Martin was aged sixty-nine in the year 1923: that is, he was born in 1854. According to Sir Frederick Jackson, in his *Uganda Early Days*, Martin was born in 1857. According to the official marriage certificate issued by the British Consulate in Zanzibar in 1896, Martin was born in 1860. No trace of his Certificate of Birth has been found in Malta although there is a reference to his birth in Il-Marsa, Malta, in 1857.

Notes

1. *Odnadwy Nos* (Fateful Night) is the title of a book about the shipwreck by T. Llew-Jones.

2. There is evidence of a Mr Frederick Smith, who came to Malta on the HMS *Success* as a sailmaker back in in 1805 and then worked in dry dock in Malta. It is speculated that he later left the dry dock to set up his own factory, which his son had by this time taken over.

3 J. Keenan, art. 48, para. VI, p. 48.

4. A brief account of the works of Mons Paolo Pullicino by J. B. Cassar, University of Malta, 1953.

5. Tim Jeal, *Stanley*, p. 35

6. Tim Jeal, *Stanley*, p. 15.

7. Kapuscinski, *The Shadow of the Sun*, p. 2

8. Alpers, *East African Slave Trade*.

9. Thomson, *Through Masai Land,* 1893

10. Thomson, *Through Masai Land,*1893.

11. Kapuscinski, *The Shadow of the Sun.*

12. Jeal, *Stanley*, p. 4.

13. From a passage in Nicholls, *Red Strangers*, p. 5; also with reference to Google Earth.

14. Nicholls, *Red Strangers*, p. 6.

15. Nicholls, *Red Strangers*, p. 33.
16. Nicholls, *Red Strangers*, p. 38.
17. Nicholls, *Red Strangers*, p. 23.
18. Nicholls, *Red Strangers*, p. 76.
19. Nicholls, *Red Strangers*, p. 47.
20. . Partridge, *The Unsung Hero*, p. 111

Acknowledgements

My parents particularly my father who discovered and resourced the basic elements of this biography, are happily remembered.

The many other people, like James Martin; missionaries, administrators (my father being one) engineers, educators, medical and other professionals, businessmen etc.etc. who spent much of their lives in the cause of developing East Africa. They shared similar experiences.

Bibliography

Alpers, Edward A., *East African Slave Trade,* Nairobi, 1967.

Bell, Hesketh, *Glimpses of a Governor's Life*, Sampson Low, Marston & Co., London, 1946.

Blake, George, *B.I. Centenary 1856–1956*, George Blake/Collins, London, 1956.

Bradford, Ernle, *The Great Siege: Malta 1565*, Wordsworth, 1999.

Cassar, J. B., *A Brief Account of the Works of Mons. Paolo Pullicino*, University of Malta Thesis, 1953.

Cauchi, N., *Maltese Migration in Australia*, Malta, 1990.

Cooke, Sir Albert, *Uganda Memories 1897–1940*, The Uganda Society, Kampala, 1945.

Davis, Ronald D., *The Gift of Dyslexia*, Souvenir Press, 2007.

Dawson, E. C., *Bishop Hannington: First*

Bishop of Eastern Equatorial Africa, Seeley & Co., 1887.

Filippi, Filippo de, *Le Ruwenzori*, French translation by A. Poizat.

Gray, Sir John, 'Mutesa in Buganda, 1857–1924', *Uganda Journal*, Vol. I, No. 2.

Hill, M. F., *Permanent Way: The Story of the Kenya & Uganda Railway*, E.A.R.& H., Nairobi, 1949.

Hobley, C. W., *Kenya: From Chartered Company to Crown Colony*, H. F.& G. Witherby, London, 1929.

Horden, Charles, *Military Operations. East Africa. History of the Great War*, HMSO, London, 1949.

Hunter, J.A., and Dan Mannix, *African Bush Adventures*, Hamish Hamilton, London, 1954.

Huxley, Elspeth, *White Man's Country*, Macmillan & Co., London, 1935.

Ingrams, W.H. *Zanzibar: Its History and Its*

Peoples, H. F. & G. Witherby, London, 1931.

Jackson, Sir Frederick, Early Days in East Africa, Edward Arnold & Co., London, 1930.

Jeal, Tim, *Stanley: The Impossible Life of Africa's Greatest Explorer*, Faber and Faber, 2007.

Jeal, Tim, *Livingstone,* Yale University Press, 2013.

Kapuscinski, Ryszard, *The Shadow of the Sun: My African Life*, Penguin Books, London, 1998.

Lyne, Robert Nunez, *An Apostle of Empire: Life of Sir Lloyd, William Mathews*, Allen & Unwin Ltd, London, 1936.

Macdonald, J. A. L., *Soldiering and Surveying in British East Africa*, Edward Arnold, London, 1897.

Marshall David, *History of the Maltese Language in Local Education*, Malta

University Press, 1971.
Mason, A. T., *Nandi Resistance to British Rule 1890–1906*, E.A. Publishing House, Nairobi, 1972.
Miller, Charles, *The Lunatic Express*, Macdonald & Co., London, 1972.
Nicholls, C.S., *Red Strangers: The White Tribe of Kenya*, Timewell Press Ltd, 2006.
Obama, Barack, *Dreams from My Father*, Canongate, 2007.
Pakenham, Thomas, *The Scramble for Africa 1876–1912*, Wiedenfeld & Nicolson, London, 1992.
Partridge H. J, *The Unsung Hero*, PEG Ltd, 2002.
Patterson, J. P., *The Man Eaters of Tsavo*, London, 1934.
Patterson, Bruce D., The Lions of Tsavo, McGraw-Hill, 2004
Perham, Margery, *Lugard: The Years of Adventure 1858–1898*, Collins, 1956.
Pullicino Philo, *The Road to Rome,* MPI

Publishing, 2011.

Pullicino, Philo and Mark Pullicino, *Opening Africa,* MPI publishing, Great Britain 2008.

Rotberg, Robert, *Joseph Thomson and the Exploration of Africa*, Chatto & Windus, London, 197l.

Royal Geographical Society, *Geographic Journal*, Vol. LXVI, No.1 (July 1925).

Smith, Mackenzie & Co. Ltd, *History of W. Boyd & Co*., W. Boyd & Co. Ltd, Nairobi,1949.

Snoxall, R. A., 'James Martin (Antonio Martini), 1857–1924', *Uganda Journal*, Vol. I, No. 2.

Thomas, H. B. and R. Scott, *Uganda*, Oxford University Press, 1935.

Thomson, Joseph, *Through Masai Land*, Sampson Law, Marston, Searle & Rivington, London 1893.

Marshall A Yokell, *The Treaty of Helgoland–Zanzibar:*

The beginning of the end for the Anglo-German Friendship, University of Richmond, 2010.

Vandeleur, Seymour, *Campaigning in the Upper Nile and Niger*, Methuen & Co., London, 1898.

Vasco, André, *Zanzibar sans les esclaves: La fin du Ramadhan a Zanzibar*, Leopoldville, 1954.

Willoughby, Sir John, *East Africa and its Big Game*, Longmans, Green & Co., London, 1889.

In addition, the following documents and correspondence were consulted:

Uganda Journal, Vol. I, No. 2, Staff List for 1895.

Uganda Journal, Vol. XXIII (reprinted at Invicta Press, Headley Brothers Ltd, 189 Kingsway, London),

'Captain Eric Smith's Expedition to Lake Victoria in 1891' by H. B. Thomas.

Uganda Journal, Vol. XXIII, No. 2, 'George Wilson and Dagoretti Fort' by H. B. Thomas.

Kenya Weekly News, Nakuru, 20 and 27 September 1957, 'Little Martin' by Rosa Walker.

East African Railways & Harbours Magazine, Vol. II, No. 9 (June 1956), pp. 291–3, 'The Development of Nakuru' by Mervyn Hill.

Zanzibar Gazette, 18 May 1892.

Despatch from Sir John Kirk to the Earl of Roseberry, 5 June 1886.

White Fathers: Diaries, Letters and Reports on the Missions of the Province of the White Fathers (1891–1894), General House of the White Fathers, Rome.

Letters and research papers exchanged between Eldoma Winkler (daughter of James Martin), Dr Louis Galea, Sir John Gray, H. B. Thomas and Philip Pullicino.

Standing: J. de Silva, Charles Kitchen, Francis Dugmore, **Seated:** Charles law, Elvira Martin, Frank Hall, **on ground**: J.Martin

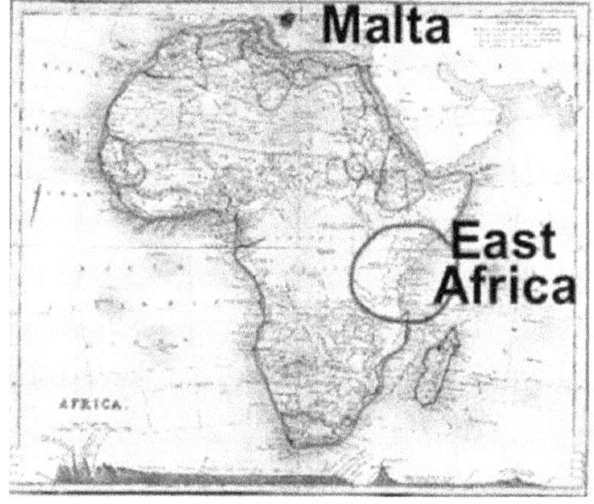

Map of East African area explored by James Martin

The Obama Tribe Explorer

Martin's Journeys in East Africa

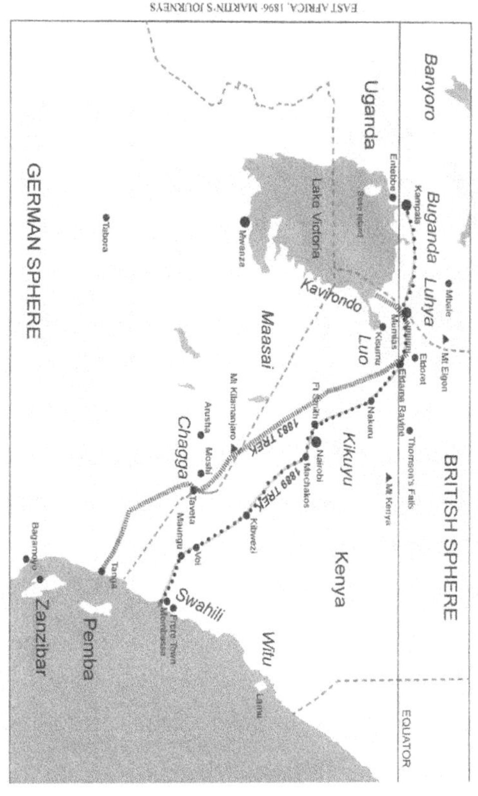

Early treks into inland Africa

Stuffed display- the “Man Eaters of Tsavo”

Shipwreck in the late 1800's

Barak Obama's Luo relatives

James Martin 1896

www.ingramcontent.com/pod-product-compliance
Ingram Content Group UK Ltd.
Pitfield, Milton Keynes, MK11 3LW, UK
UKHW020223250726
13967UKWH00001B/154

9 780954 490669